CU01503633

The New Experts

If right-populists have had enough of establishment experts, how do they replace them, with whom, and to what effect? Presenting the first in-depth analysis of India's new intellectual elite in the wake of a Hindu nationalist government, *The New Experts* investigates the power of appointed experts in normalising ideologies of governance, beyond party rhetoric. *The New Experts* presents an accessible narrative of how and why particular ideas gain prominence in elite policy and political discourse. Drawing on in-depth interviews and ethnographic research with national and international policymakers, politicians, bureaucrats, consultants, and journalists, this book analyses how political leaders in India strategically use modes of populist spectacle and established technocratic institutions to produce shared visions of glorified technological and hyper-nationalist futures.

ANURADHA SAJJANHAR is an assistant professor in Politics and Public Policy at the University of East Anglia, United Kingdom. She was a postdoctoral fellow in Policy and Governance at the Crawford School of Public Policy, Australian National University, and received her PhD from the Department of Sociology at the University of Minnesota.

The New Experts

Populist Elites and Technocratic
Promises in Modi's India

ANURADHA SAJJANHAR

CAMBRIDGE
UNIVERSITY PRESS

Shaftesbury Road, Cambridge CB2 8EA, United Kingdom

One Liberty Plaza, 20th Floor, New York, NY 10006, USA

477 Williamstown Road, Port Melbourne, VIC 3207, Australia

314–321, 3rd Floor, Plot 3, Splendor Forum, Jasola District Centre, New Delhi – 110025, India

103 Penang Road, #05-06/07, Visioncrest Commercial, Singapore 238467

Cambridge University Press is part of Cambridge University Press & Assessment, a department of the University of Cambridge.

We share the University's mission to contribute to society through the pursuit of education, learning and research at the highest international levels of excellence.

www.cambridge.org
Information on this title: www.cambridge.org/9781009349727

DOI: 10.1017/9781009349765

First published 2024

A catalogue record for this publication is available from the British Library.

Library of Congress Cataloging-in-Publication Data
Names: Sajjanhar, Anuradha, author.
Title: The new experts : populist elites and technocratic promises in Modi's India / Anuradha Sajjanhar.
Description: Cambridge, United Kingdom ; New York, NY : Cambridge University press, 2024. | Includes bibliographical references and index.
Identifiers: LCCN 2023053475 (print) | LCCN 2023053476 (ebook) | ISBN 9781009349727 (hardback) | ISBN 9781009349758 (paperback) | ISBN 9781009349765 (ebook)
Subjects: LCSH: Populism–India. | Technocracy–India. | Expertise–Political aspects–India. | Elite (Social sciences)–Political activity–India. | Modi, Narendra, 1950- | India–Politics and government–2014-
Classification: LCC JQ281 .S244 2024 (print) | LCC JQ281 (ebook) | DDC 320.56/620954–dc23/eng/20240108
LC record available at https://lccn.loc.gov/2023053475
LC ebook record available at https://lccn.loc.gov/2023053476

ISBN 978-1-009-34972-7 Hardback
ISBN 978-1-009-34975-8 Paperback

Contents

Acknowledgements   *page* vii

1   Introduction: Building Blocks   1
    Marvel of Modern Technology and Ancient Heritage   1
    Technocracy and Populism: Can They Work Together?   4
    Modi's Techno-Populist Formations   9
    Chapter Outline   13
    In Closing   15

2   The BJP's Ideological Heterodoxy   17
    Legitimacy through Multiplicity   20
    Basics of Hindutva Ideology   28
    Persuasion, Personalisation, and Propagation   35
    Conclusion   58

3   Replacing the Custodians of Discourse   60
    'Scream Fascism'   60
    The Rise of Think Tank Governance   66
    Think Tanks as Custodians of New Discourse   69
    A Typology of Indian Think Tanks   78
    Conclusion: Demos and Technos   93

4   Outsourcing Democracy through
    Professional Consulting   94
    Who Governs   94
    Policy Market   102
    Election Market: 'Ideologically Agnostic'   113
    Conclusion   131

5   The Double-Sidedness of Hindutva: Inside the BJP's
     Think Tanks   133
     The Double-Sidedness of Hindutva   137
     Inside the Think Tanks: Spatial Organisations and
         Consensus-Building   141
     Outside the Think Tank: Outreach and Education   153
     Conclusion   160

     Conclusion: Reading Indian Apolitics   162

     Works Cited   167
     Index   185

Acknowledgements

While spending the first few years of academia caught in between theories of agential autonomy and structural determinism, certain people, texts, and moments have shown me the intellectual importance of recognising contradictions therein. People, institutions, and behaviours are not pinned to their structures, nor acting in a vacuum of them – at several points, we are caught in between. Similarly, in reflecting on what it takes to make a book, I find that we are at once caught between isolation and collaboration, competition and friendship, *solitaire* and *solidaire*, instrumentality and intellectual generosity. Mostly, though, there are people who have allowed me to find safehouses that almost always lean into friendship, solidarity, collaboration, and intellectual inspiration.

I would like to thank all the people who were gracious enough to share their time, wisdom, and expertise with a persistent doctoral scholar: Yamini Aiyar, Samarth Bansal, Jairam Ramesh, Sachin Rao, M. K. Rasgotra, Rohan Sandhu, Arun Sharma, Kritika Singh, Dr Didar Singh, Harsha Vardhana Singh, Dr Subir Gokarn, Dr S. Y. Quraishi, and so many others – thank you for being such generous interlocutors and taking the time to discuss many of these burgeoning ideas with me, despite our potential disagreement. Thanks to the staff and researchers at the Centre for Policy Research, Observer Research Foundation, and (what I call) the Chanakya Institute for allowing me to be a part of your teams.

The intellectual community I developed at my brief postdoctoral time in Australian National University was immensely supportive, particularly Andy Kennedy, Azad Bali, and Shameem Black. The Interdisciplinary Center for the Study of Global Change (ICGC) community and Sociology department at the University of Minnesota provided an immersive, thoughtful, and bustling doctoral home, without which my graduate experience would have been sorely lacking. Teresa Gowan, my dear co-advisor, confidante, and friend – you are the thinker and teacher I aspire to be. Michael Goldman and Rachel Schurman – you provided intellectual and physical warmth when I most needed it. Vinay Gidwani – you are such a generous thinker, and have been an immense intellectual inspiration to me. I am grateful to Rachel Blaifeder, Lucy Rhymer, and the team at Cambridge University Press for making this book a reality, and to Harshad Marathe for the beautifully menacing cover art.

To my friends across borders and boundaries, I am lucky to know you. You have made me who I am (sorry), intellectually, politically, and sentimentally: Pallavi Agarwal, Tanja Andic, Brandi Cornelius, Christine Delp, Apoorva Gautam, Ellie Gills, Aakash Joshi Amber Joy Powell, Ellie Kuper-Thomas, Seen-Wai Lavelle, Victoria Piehowski, Marie Thouaille, Leki Thungon, Kavina Upadhyay, Benjamin Vinito, Madison van Oort.

For my family, Ashok, Madhu, and Gaurav Sajjanhar, and Meera Samaddar – you have given me endless love, freedom, and support and, to add to all that, you have (quite literally) given me the world. To Michael Sienkowski – you are my companion in transcending worlds. Thank you for the eternal support, cups of chai, laughter, and for Bodhi & Byron.

'Studying up' is an oddly mirroring exercise, as researchers often study the very communities they have an intimate familiarity with: their families, friends, colleagues, and loved ones. In this book, I focus on features of Hindutva's 'ideological strategy that are specific and important' (Hall 1985, 121), and invite collaboration that draws insight from this analysis to other arenas of struggle and solidarity. I hope I do justice to the people, structures, and contradictions at play in this crucial political moment. I also hope that this contributes, in some way, to a growing corpus of knowledge on strategies of the powerful. All mistakes, misrepresentations, and lapses of clarity are entirely my own and indicative of ideas that are growing and in flux.

Introduction
Building Blocks

MARVEL OF MODERN TECHNOLOGY AND ANCIENT HERITAGE

In December 1992, the front page of the *Times of India* diagnosed the Indian republic as irreversibly 'besmirched'. The sequence of events prompting this prognosis centred on the Babri Masjid: a mosque that was built in the sixteenth century and, according to members of the Hindu-nationalist 'family' of groups (the Sangh Parivar), sat atop the birthplace of Lord Ram, a mythical deity from the ancient epic Ramayana. They demanded the 'liberation' of Ram's holy birthplace from its centuries of Muslim suppression. Bharatiya Janata Party (BJP) leader L. K. Advani led a public march from Gujarat to Ayodhya to mobilise support for the *Ram Janmabhoomi* [Ram's birthplace] movement. This erupted in the mob-fuelled demolition of the Babri Masjid in 1992 and catalysed waves of vitriol and inhuman brutality against Muslims across the country. The prime minister at the time, P. V. Narasimha Rao, temporarily banned the RSS,[1] the BJP's grassroots paramilitary organisation. Yet an interview with a member of the RSS at the time showed them unperturbed. The government might ban the organisation, he said, but it cannot stem the spread of their ideas (Rattanani 2020).

In 2019, almost three decades later, the Supreme Court of India declared that the 1992 demolition may have been illegal, but the disputed land now belonged to Lord Ram. The then Chief Justice of India, Ranjan Gogoi, noted, 'The land rights of the disputed 2.77

---

[1] The Rashtriya Swayamsevak Sangh (RSS) is a Hindu paramilitary organisation, roughly translating to National Volunteer Organisation.

acre land will be handed over to the deity Ram Lalla, who is one of the three litigants in the case' (Firstpost 2019).

On 5 August 2020, construction of the Ram Mandir over the ruins of the Babri Masjid began ceremoniously. Prime Minister Modi led a *bhoomi pujan* (prayer) by laying a fifty-pound silver brick at the construction prayer site (Singh 2020). Despite a surge of coronavirus cases in India, crowds waving saffron flags and chanting 'Jai Shri Ram' [Hail Lord Ram] flanked the area. National newspapers circulated photographs of women in burqas and hijabs performing an *aarti* prayer over pictures of Lord Ram as they celebrated the groundbreaking of the temple. Elsewhere in the country, crowds gathered to watch live public screenings of the event (The Financial Express 2020). In New York's Times Square and Washington, DC's Capitol Hill, organised members of the Indian diaspora gathered to celebrate this momentous occasion. If the symbolism of building a Hindu temple over a destroyed mosque left any room for doubt, the then president, Ram Nath Kovind, tweeted, 'Felicitations to all for the foundation laying of Ram Temple in Ayodhya. Being built in tune with law, it defines India's spirit of social harmony and people's zeal. It will be a testimony to ideals of RamRajya and a symbol of modern India'. Modi compared the moment to India's Independence Day, announcing that the statue of Ram, which has, thus far, been 'staying in a tent', will now have a grand temple as a 'modern symbol of Indian culture' (Firstpost 2020).

India has long been lauded as the largest democracy in the world, prompting international commentators to celebrate its multiple religious communities and describe its elections as feats of far-reaching and inclusive representation. Yet, over the last decade, an increasingly ethno-nationalist leadership has eroded this global image. The BJP's rhetoric following the construction of the Ram Mandir is predictably victorious. However, the mirrored language of the Congress Party (the BJP's main political opposition and the party that amended the Indian Constitution to add the word 'secular' in 1975) demonstrates how Hindu nationalism has become a mediating discourse across political party elites lines[2] (Reddy 2011a). The Congress Party's former General Secretary, Priyanka Gandhi Vadra, called the event a hopeful 'marker of national unity, brotherhood and cultural harmony in accordance with the message of Lord Ram and with his blessings' (Indian Express 2020).

While the Ram Mandir was one of the BJP's key election promises in 2014 and 2019 and featured heavily in their manifesto, it has become a matter of shared political aspiration, cultural nationhood, and technological modernity. More recently, the Ram Mandir has promised to include high-tech security systems and technological advances showcasing the global reach of the Ramayana, constituting both a 'marvel of modern technology and ancient heritage' (Digital Desk 2021). In 2020, a prominent self-described 'liberal right of centre' news portal 'catering to the new India' published an article accusing establishment intellectuals, historians, and archaeologists of intellectual dishonesty in opposing the Ram Janmabhoomi movement (Mehta 2020). This piece asserted that such left-liberal intellectuals had 'damaged the social fabric of India' by arguing that the Babri Masjid was illegally demolished and that there was no evidence of it being built on top of Hindu ruins. At the discovery of Hindu iconography and religious structures underneath the site, a new set of right-wing experts have reinforced their legitimacy, both cultural and political, to build the Ram Mandir on the ruins of the mosque.

The evolving discourse on the building of the Ram Mandir is emblematic of how notions of technological modernity and technocratic expertise[3] interact with deep-rooted historical disputes and

---

[2] In many ways, Hindu nationalism has been a core undercurrent of Indian nationalism for the last eight decades, constituting key slogans and normative ideals of the Independence movement and beyond. See Chapter 2 for more on how, more recently, the BJP has been able to carve out mainstream acceptability for its world view.

[3] I understand technocracy as encompassing a discourse of rational governance, set of institutions, bureaucratic practices, pragmatically oriented technical experts, and a culture of corporate professionalism. While I am not conflating technological advances with technocratic expertise, claims to the former are often a close companion of the latter.

identities to create a distinct political assemblage in contemporary India. While discrediting, attacking, and replacing existing policy-makers, experts, and intellectuals they consider to be brainwashed by left-liberal establishment rhetoric, the Indian right wing has been developing its own set of institutional bodies to legitimise their presence in elite political, cultural, and policy conversations.

This book is, at its core, motivated by a desire to map this diverse formation through an examination of (a) institutions that have become a constituent part of democratic governance: think tanks, consulting firms, IT cells, government advisory groups, political parties and (b) the multiple discourses they create, entwining populist mobilisation, technocratic governance, and the haze of anti-establishment sentiment that surrounds them. Through the first in-depth analysis of India's new intellectual elite in the wake of its Hindu supremacist government, I argue that technocratic and populist discourse can work together to produce shared visions of glorified technological and hyper-nationalist futures. Simply put, I ask the question: if right-populists have had enough of establishment experts, how do they replace them, with whom, and to what effect?

While presenting itself as anti-establishment, Modi's particular populist formation engages in strategies to appeal to a wide range of demographics while replacing the old elite with a new set of legitimised experts.

TECHNOCRACY AND POPULISM: CAN THEY WORK TOGETHER?

I start with a fundamental tension within democratic formations: should societies be governed by the people, or by the experts? Political movements that claim to embody the 'people' as the backbone of their visions for social change have historically spanned the left/right ideological spectrum, and often put themselves in opposition to insular and elite experts. This binary is rife throughout hegemonic political movements, ranging from Nazi Germany in the 1930s, McCarthy's 'Red Scare' hunt for US communists in the

1950s, Mao's Cultural Revolution in the 1960s, a Thatcherite dismissal of left-liberal intellectuals in the United Kingdom in the 1980s, to President Trump's call to diminish institutional intellectuals in the United States in 2016.

In the 1960s, for example, Richard Hofstadter recognised a virulent strain of anti-intellectualism in his seminal work, *Anti-Intellectualism in American Life*. He wrote with shock and dismay at the Republican Party's treatment of so-called egghead intellectuals, positing that it was driven wholly by a 'resentment of the life of the mind, and those who are considered to represent it; and a disposition to constantly minimise the value of that life' (Hofstadter 2012). Hofstadter assigned anti-intellectualism to a rise in utilitarianism and 'the cult of the practical or self made man' (Peters 2019, 357), or a 'mystique of practicality' (Masciotra 2014). In India, forms of anti-intellectualism have encompassed religious fervour, anti-elitism, and technocratic instrumentalism, often overlapping and interacting in dissonant ways. Since the 2014 national election, a distaste against intellectuals has served to discredit several of India's public intellectuals, citing insularity due to their upper-middle-class lifestyle, English-medium education and proficiency, lack of business or corporate experience, or their institutional/personal networks (Yadav 2020). Hindu nationalists have mobilised this anti-elite discourse alongside the religious fervour of Hindu-nationalist politics. For example, terms like 'Khan Market gang',[4] 'sickular' (a play on secular), 'anti-national', and 'Tukde Tukde Gang'[5] emerged over the last ten years out of instances caricaturing or targeting different combinations of dissenting academics, students, intellectuals, and left-liberals.

---

[4] Khan Market is an elite area of South Delhi where liberal intellectuals, expats, and others of the upper-middle-to-upper classes give regular patronage to gourmet restaurants, bookshops, and designer stores (Mehta 2019).

[5] Tukde Tukde Gang literally translates to 'the breaking-up gang', used by people to refer to the students at Jawaharlal Nehru University who protested the government's occupation in Kashmir in 2016 as 'breaking up' the unity of India.

Of course, populist resentment against the Indian and often-times global elite is not without cause. The ability to make decisions and access economic, political, and cultural capital has long been limited to increasingly smaller groups of powerful people. Many articles and books have been published on the global spate of populist movements in the last decade (see Berezin 2009; Bickerton and Accetti 2021; Buštíková 2019; Moffitt 2016; Muller 2021; Wodak 2015). These works do the essential service of analysing how these movements can bolster hyper-nationalist sentiments, neoliberal governance, and/or the rise of authoritarian leaders.

Yet few of these books address whether these movements have accompanied technocratic promises of efficiency, governance, and pragmatic delivery. When they do, scholars have primarily focused on the United States, the United Kingdom, or Europe and identified heightened technocracy as an elite reaction or a rational corrective to populist demands. Recently, Bickerton and Accetti (2021) conceptualised the phenomenon of 'techno-populism' as a dominant political logic in contemporary societies that prompts political actors to appeal to 'the people' while promising bureaucratic efficiency. Crucially, they argue that the rise of techno-populism in the latter half of the twentieth century has replaced and/or overlain traditional paradigms of substantive group interests and partisan ideological commitments. Through a deep focus on India, I show how populism and technocratic expertise can offer promises not, as Bickerton and Accetti suggest, unmoored from party ideology but instead *grounded* in traditional group interests, partisan politics, and organised ideological frameworks.

As such, the Indian case challenges broader theories of populism: namely, that populist actors do not always emerge from outside political establishments and in opposition to established technocratic institutions. Rather, I demonstrate how populism can effectively dovetail with, rather than against, technocratic promises of governance through a new breed of elite experts. Beyond India under Modi, there are historical precedents to this claim: Italy under Mussolini and Britain under Thatcher similarly offered a homogenous national identity while promising to deliver goods and services to 'the people' more efficiently, without bureaucratic stagnation. Establishment groups, then, can mobilise and undermine traditional political apparatuses to combine these two strange bedfellows: technocratic expertise and populist anti-elitism.

Indeed, populist and technocratic appeals to legitimacy can be tied to policies from any end of the political spectrum (Centeno 2010). Bickerton and Accetti (2021) identify 'techno-populist' parties in Western Europe to argue that the dominant terms of political competition have shifted away from a model where politics represented existing religious, regional, and economic cleavages. This has been replaced, or overlain, by a model where parties win based on who can more successfully combine 'populist claims to represent the people as a whole with the technocratic competence to design and implement effective policy' (Bickerton and Accetti 2021, 36). All parties represent themselves as 'catch-all' (Bickerton and Accetti 2021, 91) entities, becoming ideologically neutral purveyors of policy for an apparent common good. Yet, unlike the Five Star Movement (M5S) in Italy or Macron's La République En Marche (LREM) movement in France, the BJP is, at its core, historically premised on representing a specific social identity. While this becomes either heightened or diluted in its different manifestations, Hindu supremacy remains as central to the BJP's discourse and electoral competition as technocratic competency.

India and Western Europe have significantly different histories of political party formation and pipelines into political and bureaucratic leadership. As such, the paths by which populism and technocracy have become entwined are starkly different. Some have argued that politicians like Macron, who were trained as apolitical technocrats and used technocratic competence to legitimise their power, have subsequently embraced populist techniques to compete with radical right populists (Perottino and Guasti 2020). Macron's LREM was formed in 2016 after a Great March across France, where a tightly knit group of policy specialists surveyed what the French public wanted most. They found that French citizens were dissatisfied with the political establishment and more interested in 'consensual' policy goals (improving living standards and public order and security) rather than 'ideologically connoted political projects' (Bickerton and Accetti 2021, 44). This appeal to consensual policy goals is premised on a universalised conception of common good, untainted by seemingly partisan, religious, cultural, and social biases. Similarly, the Five Star Movement in Italy relied on the organisational, crowdsourced power of the Internet to pool competence of ordinary citizens: not as bearers of subjective interests but as individual experts and carriers of a specific competence. Both LREM and M5S represented themselves as problem-solvers rather than politicians, eschewing politics in favour of post-ideological expertise to address people's problems.

In India, however, the BJP's primary appeal is that of a mass popular party simultaneously proffering both deeply ideological and seemingly neutral, post-ideological solutions. Trade unions, religious organisations, civic associations (and more recently, social media) remain the means through which political parties, both regional and national, sustain and build support (Chhibber and Verma 2018). While economic policy frameworks across major political parties in India have remained fairly consistent since economic liberalisation in 1991 (indeed, neoliberal policies have been so written into the lexicon of 'good' public policy that they no longer appear to be ideologically tinged), there is a clear social, identitarian element to the interests of the BJP–RSS. Here, populism and technocratic claims to expertise[6]

---

[6] Indeed, I examine how technocracy does not necessarily depoliticise democratic institutions, but *politicises expertise* through electoral claims to competence.

make appeals situated within party ideology, group interests, partisan politics, and organised ideological frameworks. Yes, the 'political logic' (Bickerton and Accetti 2021, 2) of competition has changed, as, since the 1980s, the BJP has actively developed coalitions, expanded its intra-party demographics and political base beyond upper-caste Hindus, and strategically moderated some of its policy promises. But rather than shifting away from organised interests, the overall terms of electoral competition have become more majoritarian, combining Hindutva with promises of technocratic competency.

MODI'S TECHNO-POPULIST FORMATIONS

How does the BJP intelligentsia successfully hold together different, sometimes contradictory, promises and paradigms of governance? While a Hindu majoritarian nation and/or state may appear contradictory to technocracy and/or an ideal of Indic civilisational harmony, they converge across varying framings of social life. Prime Minister Modi's government offers to deliver goods and services to the people by sidestepping bureaucratic inefficiency, while simultaneously rallying the public to combine aspirations for development with desires for a unifying Hindu supremacy. As such, this book explains how the BJP and its related political and cultural associations work through a diverse set of mechanics and techniques that focus on targeting constituents with different messages.

While discrediting, attacking, and replacing left-liberal intellectuals, alternative 'right wing' intellectuals build a mimetic cultural infrastructure to legitimate their own Hindutva[7] ideology. At the

---

[7] While many assume the word Hindutva to refer to Hinduism as a 'way of life' or as Hindu-ness, Hindutva was coined by an RSS ideologue, V. D. Savarkar, in 1923 as a political ideology seeking to make Indian national identity synonymous with Hindu identity. In Savarkar's words, the term 'articulates criteria for Indian identity based on citizenship, common ancestry, common culture and regard for India as fatherland (pitrbhu) and sacred land (puṇyabhu)'. See Chapter 2 for more discussion on the ideological basis for contemporary Hindutva.

same time, glorified technical experts associated with the government and its politics project the image of apolitical objectivity, moderation, and economic pragmatism. They speak to different constituencies: explicit Hindutva supporters and/or the middle classes and professionals who may nurture a Hindu normativity but are primarily motivated by bourgeois concerns. Based on in-depth interviews and ethnographic research with national and international policymakers, politicians, bureaucrats, consultants, and journalists, this book analyses how political leaders in India strategically use modes of populist spectacle and established technocratic institutions to appeal to multiple demographics with diverse moral–political schemas.

A variety of discourses work to legitimise different kinds of institutionalised actions. At times, the BJP benefits from working within procedural systems of government, whereas at other times it outside legality through its networks with the RSS. While one tactic of persuasion might involve personalising Modi as a leader through targeted technological tools, another, such as in their think tanks, relies on depersonalising the BJP's knowledge claims to make it seem objectively authoritative. On the campaign trail, Modi used hologram projectors on visits to urban constituencies, and vans outfitted with LCD screens to visit villages (Jaffrelot 2015). Policy rhetoric may emphasise statist paternalism to appease protectionist RSS supporters and rural constituencies demanding agricultural support, electricity, and water, while weakening labour laws, and easing land acquisition laws to please big business communities. In 2020, the Modi government introduced a series of new Farm Bills to remove the allocation of a government-subsidised Minimum Support Price for several essential grains, while still announcing unequivocal support for the farmer.

Techno-managerialism and economic centrism[8] can and have been argued to be ideologically incoherent with Hindutva politics, or a

[8] Chhibber and Verma (2018) argue that the conventional European left-right paradigm of politics (free-market liberalism on the right and state intervention on the left) often falls short of describing post-Independence Indian politics. In India, they note that both Congress Party and BJP voters hold traditionally right-wing economic

moderating force to 'balance' extreme majoritarianism (Varshney 2014). For example, Modi's initial campaign appeal to development and economic growth in 2014 led many to erase his history of participation in genocide, believing that the moderating effect of his economic policies would render the latter irrelevant. In 2015, public intellectual and historian Ramachandra Guha wrote a piece entitled 'Where are all the right-wing intellectuals?' (Guha 2015), charting a post-Independence history of left-liberal thought in Indian universities. Guha argued that the Indian right wing has tended to produce more ideologues (active in television, newspapers, and social media) than credible intellectuals. Guha quotes Ashok Desai, a former economic advisor to the government, as saying, 'No respectable economist has Hindu nationalist inclinations: the ideology is mistaken according to economics' (Guha 2015).

This assumed disjunction between economic respectability and right-wing nationalism is deeply contestable and, indeed, provenly false. The Indian 'right wing' is not a homogenous or monolithic group. Primarily because the BJP has never laid claim to a distinct political or economic ideology, the demographics of groups who support Modi and the BJP range from socially liberal to socially conservative, free-market liberal to proponents of state interventionism, protectionists to globalists, and Hindu nationalists to 'apolitical' supporters of good governance and technocratic managerialism.

Within its manifestations, discourses of Hindu nationalism present themselves through a nebulous, diffuse form that can be called on by national, local, and regional actors, sceptics, supporters, and affiliates without being necessarily connected to Hindutva's

---

values and that the two issues that separate people are: the politics of statism – that is, the extent to which the state intervenes and regulates social norms (marriage, tradition, etc.) and economic interactions (the redistribution of private property) and the politics of recognition – that is, if and how the government should address and make allowances to protect minorities (Verma 2019).

ideological core (Reddy 2011b). As such, it is able to penetrate existing idioms and vocabularies to build a generalisable nationalist ethos. While several of the BJP's statements and paradigms do contradict one another, they are able to strategically soothe these contradictions by producing shifting 'others' (economic elites/Muslims) as figures of opposition, and constructing some kind of shared commonality by positioning very different groups as 'cultural subalterns' (Gudavarthy 2018). Attitudes that privilege either technocracy or ethno-nationalist populism do not only coexist due to their shared oppositions; rather, they can symbiotically develop shared 'positive' visions of glorious technological futures, cultural harmony, and civilisational exceptionalism.

Data Sources

This book not only identifies consumers of knowledge as subjects of ambivalent ideological discourses, but also recognises that producers are subject to, and project, varied and oftentimes contradictory discourses themselves. It theorises a typology of motivations amongst prominent experts and intellectuals and examines this through several sources of rich and triangulated data. Due to the elite centralisation of political and policymaking culture in New Delhi, and the relatively recent mushrooming of think tanks (private, non-profit research organisations), their internal mechanisms have thus far been difficult to access. As such, these significant organisations of knowledge production and dissemination have escaped scholarly analysis.

Through pre-existing relationships with policy networks and elite research institutions, I draw on media sources, years of ethnographic data from working at three prominent think tanks at the heart of New Delhi, and interviews with key decision-making individuals, including members of the Economic Advisory Council to the Prime Minister (EAC-PM), the former General Secretary of the BJP, the former National Security Advisor and Indian Foreign Secretary, the former Head of Data Analytics, Indian National Congress Party, former Research Director of the BJP, former Director General of the

World Trade Organization, the director of the National Institute of Public Finance and Policy and Senior Partner of Government and Public Policy, Ernst & Young, amongst others.

CHAPTER OUTLINE

While grounded in India's empirical moment, this book addresses several urgent yet enduring questions on strategies of the right wing in altering how knowledge and expertise are produced and disseminated: how do understandings of 'expertise' and the 'people' change during moments of ideological and political transformation? How does this shape conversations surrounding what problems (and solutions) gain prominence in politics and policy discourse?

In Chapter 2, I chronologically follow the interaction between Hindutva and discourses of economic development in post-Independence political regimes. I explore how the BJP has gained legitimacy by creating multiple narratives through both technocratic organisations and populist mobilisation. Drawing on a rich literature on Hindutva's ideological basis and its interaction with economic development, this chapter introduces how the BJP adopts two distinct forms of persuasion in the pursuit of national glory: making claims about returning to an ancient cultural unity, while fixing long-persisting economic and moral decadence.

Following this foundation, Chapter 3 uses ethnographic and interview data to show how Prime Minister Modi's government oscillates between populist anti-elitism and forms of technocratic expertise to produce a distinct form of nationalism that is both seemingly pragmatic yet ethnocentric. In opposition to scholarship that sees technocracy and populism as contradictory forces, this chapter argues that they have emerged as two complementary arms of governance in contemporary India: (1) populist politics, which appeals to the masses/majority by defining nationalism through rigid boundaries of caste, class, and religion; and (2) technocratic policy, which produces a consensus of pragmatism and neutralises charges of hyper-nationalism. I emphasise the relational dynamic between the two:

they function through different, often contradictory, logics and content, yet are able to work towards the same goals in key moments of mutual reinforcement.

Chapter 4 expands Chapter 3's emphasis on techno-rationalist policymaking and populist mobilisation by tracing a rising market of professional consultants and think tanks in policymaking and political activity. Upper-caste and elite-educated men have long filled positions of power, including parliamentary seats, administrative services, business groups, advisory boards, and chambers of commerce. Despite some shifts towards caste-based affirmative action since the 1980s, the political classes remain predominantly elite (Verniers and Jaffrelot 2020). In 2014, anti-incumbent sentiment led to widespread distrust in existing experts, such that elite intellectuals and Western-educated economists holding political and policymaking positions were replaced by technical professionals: engineers, business managers, and consultants. As an alternative to intellectual and insular elites, this group of professionals projects itself as politically agnostic, rational, and a practical source of business-minded knowledge. This group, however, is no less insular or exclusionary: one set of intellectual experts has merely been replaced by a more elite, deracinated group of professional consultants situated in global management consulting firms.

Moving from technical professionals to anointed intellectuals, Chapter 5 examines the BJP's attempt to build centres of traditional intellectuals to legitimise its identity politics. While dismantling advisory committees, quashing dissent, and attacking universities and established research institutions, the BJP has built think tanks to give its political ideology a footprint in already established policy networks. Some such organisations avoid explicit association with the BJP and Hindu-nationalist groups but pursue a Hindutva agenda nevertheless. Through an ethnographic study of the BJP's two most prominent think tanks, this chapter examines how these organisations build venues for intellectual legitimacy and consolidate Hindutva networks across political, administrative, and military fields with broad implications for Indian society. Here,

I demonstrate how manifestations of Hindutva can be both explicitly political and anti-political at the same time: advocating for political interventionism while eschewing politics and forging an apolitical route towards cultural transformation.

Right-populism often sells itself on criticising established elites. But when it takes power, it ends up simply reconstructing its own versions of them. As such, this book concludes that while hyper-nationalist populist politics may appear contradictory to technocratic paradigms of governance and/or an ideal of a diffuse 'common good', a convoluted combination of these visions has become fundamental to how people make sense of their political, social, and cultural futures. Across the chapters, I show how the BJP has pursued and benefited from its ideologically ambivalent, yet persistent, project. It has been able to stitch together varying political and apolitical subjectivities through a range of persuasive strategies. In identifying the distinctive double-sidedness of Hindutva, I illuminate the knowledge-producing processes through which it has become a nebulous, diffuse logic of social life.

IN CLOSING

This book, then, traces how knowledge travels between different domains, how it gains value in public intervention and political discourse, and, finally, how certain expertise and appointed 'experts' build legitimacy for these ideas, navigating the contradictions between policy (as a technocratic exercise) and politics (as a matter of democratic legitimacy). This approach straddles political science, policy studies, and cultural studies, showing how policy organisations can build and consolidate elite networks, yet also influence cultural notions of knowledge and valued expertise. As populist movements have swept the globe, mass anti-elitism and religious anti-rationalism have often fuelled resentment of socially anointed intellectuals. Yet anger against intellectuals also stems from wanting to replace the disconnected 'eggheads' with the pragmatic businessperson and rational technocrat. In this context, cultural commentators have made pronouncements of 'the end of politics' as the result of capitalist instrumentality and economic rationalism in a range of political contexts (Dillow 2007; Mouffe 2005; Schedler 2016). Significantly, however, I urge readers not to diagnose a depoliticisation, or 'disappearance' of politics in everyday life. Rather, I determine that it is incumbent upon social scientists to pay attention to what Havelka (2016) calls *herrschaft*: ideas about how political life is organised, and how possibilities of social, cultural, and political futures are reframed.

2   The BJP's Ideological Heterodoxy

In the last five to ten years, India has seen a parallel growth of a rise of populist sentiments that seek to represent the majority, along with an era of unprecedented big-data technocracy. Populism's legitimacy is based on the ostensible 'will of the people', and technocracy on rational, primarily elite, speculation (Caramani 2017), yet, in this case, they are able to coexist. Given their seeming contradiction, scholars have argued that technological advances and techno-rationalist approaches to governance can act as correctives to identity-based majoritarianism (Rosanvallon 2011). In contrast, I show how they can often work in tandem to bolster populist claims to future glory and, indeed, expand mechanisms of state autocracy (see Chapter 3).

The Bharatiya Janata Party (BJP) has a long history of building support by targeting different constituents with different messages. At times, the party's leadership delivers business-friendly economic reforms to appeal to its corporate constituencies, or develops welfare programmes targeted to specific populations. At other times, the party uses its connection with the Rashtriya Swayamsevak Sangh (RSS), the BJP's grassroots paramilitary organisation, to incite and perpetrate Hindu majoritarian violence. At other times, the party builds concentrated forms of institutional legitimation within elite policy networks, and so on. Instead of governing based on only legal, traditional, or a singular normative notion of authority, the BJP has been able to build *multiple narratives*, using both technocratic organisations and populist mobilisation, to gain several forms of legitimacy and support, many of which contradict one another.[1] Indeed, they are

---

[1] As Suhas Palshikar has noted of the BJP in 2014, 'To its core constituency, it
continued to be a party of Hindutva; to the OBCs, it represented a vehicle of political

speaking to different constituencies: those who are ardent Hindutva supporters, to those who see it as a vehicle of political power, and to others who may nurture a Hindu normativity but are primarily motivated by possibilities of economic benefit.

Contrary to studies (Moffitt 2016; Richards 2017) which note that populist leaders come from outside the system, both Modi and the BJP–RSS network have worked both within and outside formal politics. The story of the BJP thus demonstrates how contemporary political actors can be *historically grounded in* particular interests, even though they use rhetorical, discursive, and institutional means associated with both populist and technocratic ideals.

This chapter introduces how the BJP adopts two distinct forms of persuasion, making claims about the (sometimes magnificent, sometimes repugnant) past and the future to different degrees: (1) returning to an ancient, mythic, and strategically changing cultural unity; and (2) 'cleaning up' persisting economic and moral decadence in pursuit of invulnerable national glory. I find that these mechanisms have been pursued through strategies of moderation, polarisation, personalisation, collective sacrifice, and targeted messaging. By discussing the BJP's heterodoxy, its historical significance, and its key strategies of persuasion, I show how the Indian case can challenge existing theories of populism and technocracy. This chapter provides necessary context to set up the key argument of this book: that populism can work in tandem with technocratic promises of governance through an epistemic monopoly of elite experts.

power, a vehicle articulating and absorbing their democratic upsurge; for power-seekers, it was a convenient platform offering the possibility of tactical use of the Hindutva weapon when required; for devout Hindus, it represented the religious assertion of the Hindu religion; to the new and upwardly-mobile lower-middle sections, the party represented new possibilities of economic benefit' (Palshikar 2015, 724).

I join scholars who have understood Hindutva as a mediating discourse of social life, beyond Hindutva's claims to a Hindu nation (Ludden 2005). It can be drawn on by hard-core ideologues, sympathisers, affiliates, and even critics, to strategically make their own claims not directly connected to Hindutva's ideological core. Indeed, as Verma (2019) incisively notes, political parties often develop contradictory positions when trying to expand their reach. Rather than reconciling its different messages, such as that of secular moderation with majoritarian nationalism, or state intervention with economic liberalisation, the Hindutva 'family' of organisations builds legitimacy and support through a varied set of persuasive tactics that are able to coexist despite dissonance.

This 'vernacularisation' of Hindutva logic allows political actors and communities to operationalise it in a plethora of local, national, and international contexts, such that it penetrates existing vocabularies and generates a majoritarian cultural ethos (Jaffrelot 2015; Reddy 2011a).[2] At the same time, I suggest that a persuasive strategy does not need to assume an a priori agreement between constituents and leaders. Persuasion, insofar as it is inherently communicative, relies on an iterative negotiation of making allowances, sidelining contradictions, and reframing existing beliefs. The BJP's desired result, then, may be achieved by the creation of 'alternative logics' aimed at unifying contradictory interests (Hall 1979). These logics do not necessitate a narrative coherence or even logical rationales, but allow the BJP to target specific political and economic visions to different groups without having to explain their contradictions. Simultaneously, these logics receive support and legitimacy by creating new cultural and institutional structures and infiltrating existing ones.

---

[2] For a detailed account of Modi's varying election promises on the campaign trail in 2014, see Jaffrelot (2015).

This chapter, then, considers the primary actors and socio-historical events that have led to Hindutva's multiple political imaginaries and policy imperatives. I present an analysis of the BJP's heterodoxy, followed by an overview of Hindutva's ideological basis, and a chronological tracing of how Hindutva and discourses of economic development have been co-constitutive in political regimes since the 1980s. I then arrive at the post-2014 present to argue that the BJP has historically developed a language of moral virtue, strategically using politically resonant discourse to 'sell' shifts in economic policy as symbolic, moral imperatives. I examine this through a case study of the discourses surrounding demonetisation in 2016. Chapters 3, 4, and 5 then take a closer look at key actors who fuel the multiplicities of these discourses: namely, think tanks, political consultants, consulting firms, and civil service bureaucrats.

LEGITIMACY THROUGH MULTIPLICITY

While Hindutva has experienced resurgence since 2014, Hindu nationalism has been an undercurrent of Indian nationalism for at least eight decades. Collective uprisings during the Independence movement even derived a political ethic and epistemology through fundamentally religious terms: for instance, revolutionary nationalists took oath on the Bhagavad Gita (a Hindu scripture that is part of the epic Mahabharat), and expressed allegiance to Bharat Mata (Mother India) in terms that equated Hindu nationhood with Indian nationhood (Chatterjee 1993). In its current politico-cultural manifestation, Hindutva's appeal has led to public approval of recent legal decisions to criminalise 'triple talaq',[3] dismantle

---

[3] Triple talaq refers to a practice within Muslim communities that allows Muslim men to divorce and abandon their wives by saying or writing the word 'talaq' three times. Those who campaigned to criminalise this practice on the Hindu Right did so under the guise of protecting Muslim women from being abandoned by their husbands without any accountability. While there is some validity to this argument, women's groups have also argued that criminalising this practice rather than invalidating it could prevent husbands from paying post-divorce dues, leaving their wives and children without financial security and at risk to vengeful family members

Article 370,[4] and build a Hindu temple on the site of a historically demolished mosque. Despite losing support in several state-level elections between 2019 and 2020, the BJP has still been able to pass its bills in the Rajya Sabha, the Upper House of Parliament, while only occupying a third of its seats. Beyond furthering claims towards a Hindu nation, these events demonstrate how the BJP has been able to effectively 'carve out an acceptability to its larger worldview' (Palshikar 2020). Even though opposition parties might be beating the BJP in state elections, they are increasingly sharing the same ideology, adopting similar terms of debate: for example, the 2018 Congress Manifesto in Madhya Pradesh declared the intention to develop cow shelters and commercial production of cow urine (Jaffrelot 2019).

The day after Prime Minister Modi's resounding election victory in 2019, Ram Madhav, the former National General Secretary of the BJP, published an opinion piece in a national English-medium newspaper, proudly proclaiming Modi, the leader, as having 'become' the truth. Effectively, he asserted his party's hegemonic success on a public platform:

> 'What counts is what the people think is true', Napoleon used to say. The Opposition's lies didn't cut any ice before the people's belief in Modi because of his relentless and direct engagement with them through various communication platforms. Consciously or otherwise, the Opposition has centred this election round Modi.

(Jones 2019). Instead of assuring post-divorce security, the Hindu Right's focus on criminalising triple talaq primarily targets Muslim communities and reinforces the rhetoric of Muslim women as victims of regressive Muslim men. These debates are part of a larger contention within Indian legal rights between instituting a Uniform Civil Code instead of allowing religion-specific Personal Laws.

[4] Article 370 of the Constitution, instituted by Jawaharlal Nehru, India's first prime minister, gave special status to the region of Muslim-dominated Kashmir to retain some level of autonomy, its own constitution, flag, and the right to amend its own laws. By dismantling Article 370, then, the BJP government has laid stake to Kashmir as Indian territory, ostensibly to 'bring development' to the region (BBC News 2019). Yet, in most ways, this move has led to increased military occupation, state shutdowns, curfews, and violence by the Indian state.

> And the results affirm a phenomenon that Marxist social scientist William Davies describes as 'the leader becomes the truth'.
>
> *(Madhav 2019)*

This excerpt undoubtedly announces the BJP's hegemonic *aims*.[5] The BJP and the RSS have meticulously risen to power through an 'unconditional public commitment' to liberal democratic institutions, while still effectively using organised mob violence as a tactic to gain popular support (Ahmad 2016). The RSS–BJP machinery infiltrates several social spheres. The RSS,[6] for example, calls itself a cultural organisation focused on non-governmental social work,[7] yet it is also the base of the BJP's militarised, grassroots ranks. It believes its duties are to encompass political guidance, participation, and the all-encompassing expression 'of the religion of the race' (Ahmad 2016).

Rather than a bottom-up or party-oriented mobilisation strategy, Hindutva adopts a position more diffuse and insulated from dissent (Bruff 2014). V. D. Savarkar, a chief ideologue of the RSS, coined the term 'Hindutva' to refer to a collective and unified Hindu Indian identity and held that Hinduism was not merely one of the religions of India but the Indian way of life. In this vein, the BJP lays claim to being 'truly' secular by equating Hindu with an Indian spiritual essence and universality, as opposed to the 'pseudo-secularism' of other political parties in India that ostensibly appease minorities by listening to their demands (Bonikowski 2017; Reddy 2006; Schnapper and Greaves 1994). The Ghar Wapsi ('returning home') rallies that have occurred over the last few decades aggressively proselytise that non-Hindus can be Indian only if they admit that their forefathers were Hindu and that all non-Hindus need to be 'brought back' to the

---

[5] Whether the BJP has successfully 'achieved' hegemony is debatable, as are the terms through which we can 'measure' hegemony (Jaffrelot and Verniers 2020).

[6] The RSS (the Rashtriya Swayamsevak Sangh) is a Hindu paramilitary organisation, roughly translating to National Volunteer Organisation.

[7] They present themselves as simply protecting Indian public culture, resulting in the former German Ambassador to India calling them 'one part of the mosaic that makes up India' (Haidar 2019).

Hindu way of life. Hinduism is the only native religion, they contest – thus, there is no conversion, only reconversion.

Over the last three decades, the RSS and the BJP have steadily negotiated coercion and consent – electoral politics with flagrant mob violence, legality with illegality – presenting themselves as maintaining civil liberties and upholding democratic ideals. In a post-Independence India, the RSS and Bharatiya Jana Sangh, precursor of the BJP, gained political power as 'defenders of democracy' by mobilising against Indira Gandhi's dictatorial suspension of civil liberties in the 1970s. Following the 1984 anti-Sikh riot after Indira Gandhi's assassination by her Sikh bodyguard, the RSS accelerated its tactics of organised violence and continued to gain electoral power through strategic pogroms against Muslims and minorities. Hindutva took root among the middle classes as a conservative reaction to counter the rise in political power by Dalits and lower-caste groups in the 1970s and 1980s (referred to as India's 'silent revolution' (Jaffrelot 2003)). More recently, the BJP has expanded its social base beyond upper castes and among younger segments of Dalits, tribals, and Other Backward Classes (OBCs)[8] (Desai 2014), absorbing them into the party or building political coalitions.

The BJP claims a stronghold over democratic ideals, yet has continuously undermined those to gain popular support and authority. Its fronts on the ground are countless, scattered through community organisations, *shakhas*, local political and economic bodies, and

---

[8] OBC is an administrative category given to a range of 'backward' castes in India whose ritual and occupational status are said to be 'above Dalits' but still socially and economically depressed. Yet the OBC category contains a vast expanse of social groups and castes. For example, 'there are at one extreme the dominant, landowning, peasant castes which wield power and authority over local Vaishyas and Brahmins, whereas at the other extreme are the poor, near-Untouchable groups living just above the pollution line. The category also includes many artisan and servicing castes. After cornering the benefits of this first wave of legislation, these groups attempted to block all subsequent land reform measures designed to benefit marginal farmers and the landless, who usually belonged to castes and groups lower on the social hierarchy, most notably Dalits' (Jain 2018, 136).

varied by language, caste, occupation, location, and religious sect. The RSS has long presided over a larger Sangh Parivar, a network of dispersed, national, and regional Hindu-nationalist groups that refer to themselves as a *parivar*, a family. (Anderson and Jaffrelot 2018; Jaffrelot 2007; Siddiqui 2017). The exact relationship between these organisations is unknown, and the extent to which they acknowledge their affiliation with the RSS varies (Anderson and Longkumer 2018). Nevertheless, the diversity of organisations at play comprise a broader Hindutva family and, as Anderson and Longkumer (2018) argue, in part exemplify the heterodoxy of Hindutva: whether by design (as a 'division of labour' of influencing different facets of social life (Noorani 2000)), or by unresolved and persistent internal dispute. A core contradiction within the Hindutva family is the vast number of economic and social ideologies within the BJP, the RSS, and their supporters. In a BJP press release from 2004 entitled 'Tasks Ahead', the BJP describes its vision as a clear combination of nationalism and development:

> The BJP's Vision has two focal points: Nationalism (Rashtravaad) and Development (Vikas). We believe that both are a precondition for realising our dream of a Resurgent India.
>
> *(Bharatiya Janata Party 2004)*

In trying to balance contradictory normative notions of nationalism and development, internal strands of organisations in the BJP–RSS network have vastly differing ideological roots – encompassing socially liberal libertarians; social and economic conservatives; firm believers in central governance and welfare for the 'common man'; proponents of decentralisation; followers of a World Bank–inspired 'good governance' where the state facilitates the growth of the economy; believers in a universal Hindu unity; strict adherers to hierarchical Hindu traditionalism of caste system; foreign-policy hawks; principled sceptics of the West; champions of global economic participation. Yet somehow, they all manage to form a part of the broader BJP's umbrella of supporters.

Scholars have suggested that such policy flexibility within factions of the party and its supporters is partly because Hindu nationalism has minimal allegiance to any singular economic or social ideology. For the most part, factions within Hindu-nationalist groups (and, indeed, Indian party politics as a whole) have oscillated between protectionism and pro-globalisation, both of which have, at different points in history, been supported by apparent right-wing or left-wing parties. Indeed, Modi's recent popular slogan encourages 'atmanirbhar Bharat'[9] during Covid-afflicted times, glorifying national self-reliance (as announced in a public speech on 12 May 2020).

Whether internal disputes about economic policy serve to undermine or advance the Parivar's core ideology of Hindutva nationalism is unclear. While certain commentators have seen the BJP as moving further to the centre in its embrace of globalisation and slogans of development, others argue that such a mainstream economic stance has only served to make the party as a whole, including its ethno-centric nationalism, more palatable. By oscillating between periods of moderation and polarisation, the BJP's ethno-nationalist views have become more normalised, and moved the centre of gravity further to the right (Chacko 2019; Jaffrelot 2013; Ruparelia 2006; Varshney 2014). Periods of moderation have allowed for democratic coalition building and wider resonance, while periods of polarisation have led to further anti-Muslim, Hindu majoritarian radicalisation. As such, the BJP's strategies to build support are wide-ranging and incongruent, encompassing both gestures to a discourse of globalised universality[10] as well as essentialism and particularity (see section on ' "Cleaning Up" the Economy' for further analysis).

---

[9] Atmanirbhar Bharat encourages a rhetoric to 'turn the Covid crisis into opportunity' and boycott Chinese products. The finance minister has said that this relief package does not discourage Foreign Direct Investment, or isolation from the global market.

[10] In actuality, this discourse of globalised universality conceals a strategic globalism that sees closer economic and geopolitical ties with some countries more than others, and includes caveats on India's obligation to adhere to 'global' norms, for example, on climate change, human rights, and so forth.

Hindutva and Civil Society

The Sangh Parivar's main influences across civil society have been through its unions (for workers, students, peasants, and tribals), as well as a wide range of cultural and religious civic associations, many of which fall under the aegis of 'apolitical' community-based, humanitarian, or social work. In September 2018, approximately a hundred religious practitioners ranging from public intellectuals, academics, to professionals met to demand 'Equal Rights for Hindu Communities', putting together a Charter of Hindu Demands. As of 2021, two of the charter's eight demands have been fulfilled: the abrogation of Article 370, and the decision to enact a new citizenship bill for those of practising Indian-origin religions (Hindus, Sikhs, Jains, and Buddhists) (Times of India 2020). As-yet unfulfilled demands include banning foreign funds (except those from the Indian diaspora) to Indian organisations, banning the export of beef, enacting a Freedom of Religion Act that 'prevents interference' in the 'propagation of native Hindu and Indic religious practices', and the freedom to teach Hindu cultural practices in schools without government interference (Sarayu Trust 2018).

Indeed, scholars have argued that the Sangh Parivar has gradually gained dominance because of its huge presence in a combination of 'the realm of civil society', unions, and a range of associations that 'shape public debates' (Palshikar 2019, 110). Apart from organised associations, the BJP has also worked to infiltrate popular cultural artefacts through schools, textbooks, films, and books, while simultaneously developing its own intellectual cultural infrastructure. Proponents of the Hindu Right have adopted mediums of liberal intellectual culture to disseminate its own politics: such as literary festivals, film festivals, policy conferences, panel discussions positing 'open debate', cultural festivals celebrating Indic cultures, and so on. As Srinivasaraju (2019) notes, 'The Sangh did not have a pantheon of heroes, and they made it their post-truth mandate to unabashedly borrow from liberal traditions of the literary, political and spiritual for their ideological project' (see Chapter 5 for details). In the realm of knowledge production, what Udupa (2015) calls New India's social media 'ideological army' is a significant portion of its voice in civil society. Their active presence on social media, powered through highly advanced algorithms and dedicated IT cells, has been successful at building communities of aggressive BJP followers both online and offline (Chaturvedi 2016; Udupa 2018b).

With Hindutva becoming an increasingly dominant language through which people understand political life, cosmopolitan Indians can negotiate their level of affiliation, sympathy, and critique of its various tenets. While agreeing with certain parts of it, they can detach themselves from others. This particular ambivalence and internal contradiction shapes public debate to the extent that 'the Sangh Parivar is its own opposition' (Jaffrelot and Verniers 2020, 145). The Hindu Right's voice in civil society, then, is not always explicitly linked to the BJP, Hindutva, or the Sangh Parivar. It oscillates between adopting a language of political outrage and detached calls for cultural recognition. The Charter of Hindu Demands quotes RSS leader Keshav Baliram Hedgewar on 'nourish [ing] the Hindu culture', yet otherwise makes no mention of the RSS, Hindu Rashtra, or the BJP. In Reddy's words, this 'amorphously constituted civil society group' distances itself from 'traditional Sangh Parivar logics, politics, and practices; it demands a reconfigured relationship to the State and protections for "Indic" culture' (Reddy 2018, 2).

On the landing page for the Charter of Hindu Demands website, a video of an interview with a prominent Kannada scholar discusses why, in India, 'a section of the educated and intellectual group oppose everything related to Hinduism' (Equal Rights for Hindus n.d.). He argues that people were divided on the basis of caste, divided by the British, British historians, British sociologists, and British economists. The post-Independence Congress government, he says, did 'not allow India to develop into its own country' and instead adopted a colonised mindset. Intellectuals from the Hindu Right often claim that the British (and the circa sixteenth- or seventeenth-century Muslim Mughal Empire before them) invaded and corrupted an essential Indianness. Based on this interpretation, the mimetic intellectual culture of Hindutva claims its own space in the domain of Indian traditional intellectuals, wanting to shift intellectual paradigms from within the liberal, academic elite.

Indeed, to the extent that intellectuals exert influence on 'claims about descriptions of the world, causal relationships, or the normative legitimacy of certain actions' (Parsons 2002, 48), they impact political discourse in three major ways: constructing the problems and issues that shape policy agendas; shaping social and economic assumptions that can impact the content of reform proposals, legitimising or challenging existing institutions and policies; becoming 'discursive weapons' (Béland 2009, 701) that participate in the construction of reform imperatives. In India's policy networks, experts can challenge existing institutional configurations and convince policymakers, interest groups, and the general population that change is necessary. Specific ideas are more likely to become politically influential when influential actors (such as politicians, intellectuals, and elite policymakers) decide to promote them, reifying a 'social construction of the need to reform' (Cox and Carr 2001, 464).

BASICS OF HINDUTVA IDEOLOGY

> A successful hegemonic ideology will mask contradictory interests while offering some 'unified' sense of belonging to the majority. This is where nationalism comes in, calling for subordination to a 'higher' cause or promising benefits to 'true nationals', and thereby reconciling otherwise clashing interests.
>
> (Vanaik 2018, 30)

In the 2014 and 2019 election campaigns, the BJP's internal IT cells in conjunction with hired political consulting firms put together large databases profiling citizens in each constituency according to socio-economic demographics, caste, religion, and occupation. They then created hundreds of WhatsApp groups, Facebook groups, and other forms of media and social media communication, populating them with (often fake) stories and illusions about the Congress and BJP track records – both personal and political. These messages were all targeted to their particular groups based on data on their affinities, prejudices, biases, and demands.

During the 2019 election campaign, the BJP's party cadre transmitted messages throughout towns, cities, and villages (see Chapter 4 for details). Party workers and foot soldiers worked along with two data mining organisations (Jarvis Technology and Strategy Consulting Limited, and Association of a Billion Minds), reaching out to constituents who benefited or were offered key welfare schemes (Dutta 2019). Top party leadership used the NaMo app to communicate with party workers while using social media and traditional media to address core desires appealing to material needs; symbolic needs (something to fight for – that is, national security and nationhood); aspirations of moral and material desires; and othering imagined enemies (someone to blame).

These hybrid desires and needs are addressed through a range of so-called alternative logics built on the base logic of Hindutva. An example of a WhatsApp message shared on one of the several BJP groups I joined is given below. This message from a group called 'NaMo Government' (with more than 100 participants) is targeted to members of an urban constituency in Uttar Pradesh, the most populous state in India and one in the middle of the Hindu belt. The message lists major politicians of other regional and national opposition parties, claiming that they want to appeal to Muslim voters to appease them and, thus, the BJP is the only party that cares for Hindu voters or appeals to a generalised Indian interest.

Forwarded:
Congress is asking for Muslim votes.
Communists are asking for Muslim votes.
Kejriwal is begging for Muslim votes.
Mayawati is asking for Muslim votes.

Mamata is asking for Muslim votes.

Akhilesh is asking for Muslim votes.

Laloo is asking for Muslim votes.

DMK is asking for Muslim votes.

Deve Gowda is asking for Muslim votes.

Sharad Pawar is asking for Muslim votes.

Looks like no one wants HINDU VOTES

What say Hindus? Why don't you vote for BJP which is the
only party which cares for your votes?

The majority of foundational thinkers of the RSS and Hindu nationalism in the late nineteenth century were upper-caste Brahmins. They
sought to resurrect the ancient glory of Hindus to oppose both
'Muslim usurpers' and Dalit social movements seeking to challenge
the Brahmanical caste order (Ahmad 2016). V. D. Savarkar coined the
term 'Hindutva' in 1923 to refer to a collective and unified Hindu
Indian identity and held that Hinduism was not merely one of the
religions of India but coterminous with being Indian. He argued that
religion was only part of 'Hinduness' and that territory, cultural commonality, and racial features are all necessary to define an ethnic
national identity.

The BJP and RSS have since combined Savarkar's Hindutva
ideology with the outlook of other foundational Hindu supremacist
thinkers, such as M. S. Golwalkar (leader of the RSS from 1940 to
1973) and Deendayal Upadhyaya (a member of the RSS who became
general secretary of the Jana Sangh political party in 1951, the precursor to the BJP). Golwalkar's philosophy expanded Savarkar's formulation of 'political virility' and made clear the race hatred at the core of
the RSS. He argued that Hindutva identity surpassed the state and
encompassed a collective imagination of national unity. In other
words, he understood the RSS's mission to be in service to the
Hindu *nation*, to which the political state was subordinate.
Golwalkar criticised Gandhi's nationalism for being merely a 'terri-
torial nationalism' in which nationhood and citizenship were

geographical, whereas Golwalkar preached a cultural nationalism of the Hindu 'race'. To Golwalkar, culture is synonymous with all aspects of Indian social, political, religious, and economic life (Jaffrelot 2007). As he wrote in his most influential book, *We, or Our Nationhood Defined*,

> The foreign races in Hindusthan must either adopt the Hindu culture and language, must learn to respect and hold in reverence Hindu religion, must entertain no idea but those of the glorification of the Hindu race and culture, i.e., of the Hindu nation and must lose their separate existence to merge in the Hindu race, or may stay in the country, wholly subordinated to the Hindu Nation, claiming nothing, deserving no privileges, far less any preferential treatment – not even citizen's rights.
>
> *(Golwalkar 1939, 104)*

Golwalkar, too, made clear the RSS's admiration of the Nazi party. He writes, in the same book,

> To keep up the purity of the Race and its culture, Germany shocked the world by her purging the country of the Semitic Races – the Jews … Germany has also shown how well-nigh impossible it is for Races and cultures, having differences going to the root, to be assimilated into one united whole, a good lesson for us in Hindusthan to learn and profit by.
>
> *(Golwalkar 1939, 87)*

Following Golwalkar in his role as the head of the Jana Sangh political party, Deendayal Upadhyaya cloaked the RSS's race hatred in a philosophy of 'integral humanism': seeing society as a natural living organism with a 'national soul' whose needs paralleled the needs of the individual (Bhatt 2001, 29). He was tasked with the mission of turning the Jana Sangh into a genuine member of the Hindu-nationalist *parivar* (family). With his philosophy of integral humanism, he effectively universalised metaphysical aspects of Hindu philosophy (such as *dharma* (truth or duty)) to appeal to a wider range of constituents. While he also demanded that Muslims assimilate to a Hindu India, Upadhyaya's softer rhetoric of humanistic Hindutva has become a significant part of the BJP's external self-presentation. While other religious groups can live in India, Upadhyaya said, they 'must identify themselves with the age-long national cultural stream that was Hindu culture in this country' (Kulkarni 2017).

The RSS continues to understand being Hindu not only as a religious category but also as a set of normatively established behaviours necessary to belong to the nation. Indeed, as many scholars have noted (Anderson and Longkumer 2018; Jaffrelot 1993, 2007; Palshikar 2015), it is key not to conflate the goals of the RSS with the BJP, or the BJP with the Sangh Parivar. My interviews revealed how the distinction and tension between the RSS and the BJP are plenty. For one, members of the RSS shared that the ideas and ideological foundations of the RSS are of an *Akhand Bharat*, a unified Hindu India. Rather than amassing formal political power, and expelling other religions into new states, the RSS officially pursues a 'pure', ideologically grounded, united Hindu nation that includes reclaiming Pakistan and Bangladesh. In this sense, the RSS does not necessarily want formal political power or to occupy elite institutions, but the long-term accomplishment of these goals. These tensions, as this chapter later elaborates, have emerged in the BJP's multifaceted campaigns that swing between extreme polarisation and moderation.

One of the BJP administration's strategies in recent years has been to manufacture 'moral panics' to unify fractured parts of the electorate and party. Critical theorist Stuart Hall identified 'moral panics' to understand the cultural anxiety that emerged around black criminality in the United Kingdom and distracted the public from the wider economic crisis during Prime Minister Thatcher's regime in the 1980s. More broadly, moral panics are a culturally produced fixation on a specific event or population, and are often used politically to fuel popular actions and reactions in specific directions. Hall argued that Thatcher's aims were hegemonic: to struggle to gain dominance and consent on several fronts, 'to win in civil society as well as in the state' (Hall 1985). While there are vast differences between Thatcherism and the BJP's current tenure in Indian politics, this concept is key to studying knowledge production and ideological dissemination of the contemporary Indian state. Here, it is worth recalling Reddy's characterisation of Hindutva's methods: 'If the Hindutva that Savarkar or Golwalkar once imagined exists at all, it exists as a set of tools, logics, and mechanisms by which contemporary politics at all levels plays out' (Reddy 2011b, 421) The project of the BJP, then, encompasses not only political or economic power; rather, it attempts to wage ideological struggle at the heart of morality and common sense.

The Indian experience of Hindu nationalism has shown that constitutional democracy, instead of increasing pluralism and tolerance, can also give way to authoritarian and anti-democratic majoritarian movements. As Urbinati (2019) has noted, populism can use and change representative democracy. It can mobilise the cornerstone of democratic legitimacy (i.e. the power of the people) against its minorities and political opposition, thus disfiguring it into an extreme form of majoritarianism. The RSS has expressed historical condemnation of the mandate laid out by the Constitution, yet has managed to utilise its modes of liberal democracy to effectively rise to power through the BJP (Ahmad 2016). Golwalkar (1966) has famously written:

> Our Constitution too is just a cumbersome and heterogeneous piecing together of various articles from various Constitutions of Western countries. It has absolutely nothing, which can be called our own. Is there a single word of reference in its guiding principles as to what our national mission is and what our keynote in life is? No!
>
> *(Shamsul-islam 2010, 10)*

The 'deep state' of Hindutva (Anderson and Jaffrelot 2018) is thus made not only of those within the state apparatus but also those in the street who perform lynchings and mass mob attacks on Muslims, Dalits, and other minorities, with impunity. While these activities might be *illegal*, they are *legitimate* for Hindu nationalists, and legitimacy is able to trump legality in the imagination of the Hindu nation. Another WhatsApp group for constituents in a North Delhi neighbourhood called 'Nationalist Vande Mataram' shares a message that furthers a sensation of Hindu victimhood and a future Hindutva imaginary:

> Most Hindus have been enlightened now, aware of what's happening & getting united & fighting back. The blame game by Muslims in India & Christian constitutional countries is just a farce. Kudos to Hindus. Unification of Hindus has been successful to quite an extent. Braver & stronger.

> One day India will get it's [sic] original name Bharatvarsh & the unjust laws against Hindus will be removed, the Kashmiri Pandits who were tortured & removed from their own land will get their houses back, Christian mafia & Naxals will end, Gazwa-e-Hind chapter will be shut down forever, with hanging of all those who initiated it. Schools & Temples will teach the actual original culture of Bharat & Sanskrit will be compulsory in all schools of India. The Christian missionary schools & Christian ashrams with their conversion rackets will end. We will then see a wholly united Bharatvarsh & no South North or Language divide; instead reaping the fruits of our original Culture & understanding each other.

Here, a range of languages, regions, religions, and political groups are swiftly turned into discursive tools that position Hindus as the basis of an 'original culture'. An emphasis on unity, primarily Hindu-enforced unity, seeks to erase 'language divides'; Christian groups and schools are referred to as 'mafias'; and Muslims, Christians, and Naxals (which refers to both the Maoist political group and as a euphemism for leftist-liberal dissenters) are othered with disdain.

PERSUASION, PERSONALISATION, AND PROPAGATION

Melding Hindutva with Development

During the 2014 and 2019 national elections, tensions between the BJP's Hindutva and its inclusive development-focused campaign narratives were evident, but were able to coexist by appealing to different target demographics while satisfying different desires. In the 2022 state elections, Modi spoke at a rally in Goa identifying the BJP with development and other parties with identitarian violence: 'New parties are coming to Goa to launch their political aspirations. Goans have sent them a message to keep their violence to themselves, Goans will choose development' (Times of India 2022). My interviews with policymakers also revealed their perception that a handful of BJP–RSS leaders might espouse anti-Muslim anger and Hindu state sentiments, but what they 'do' never reflects that discrimination (i.e. in tangible policy implementation). They assert that the public ought to judge the BJP on the latter.

> In terms of impressions, despite counterintuitive facts, BJP is [still seen as] a Hindu party. That branding is refusing to go away [because of] jokers within the party and outside, all this RSS stuff. To me, the development discourse is visible. I can see it. Look at the roads, they've tripled, as in, kilometres per day – check the numbers and you'll see. Check Ayushman Bharat. I think if you look at any metric, [Modi's] doing fine. Data is the metric that you must lean on.
>
> *(Interview with representative from Observer Research Foundation,[11] leading New Delhi think tank, March 2019)*

In the last decade and particularly since the run-up to Modi's election in 2014, Hindu nationalism has seemingly coupled its tactics with development goals (Palshikar 2015; Vanaik 2017). Development, both economic and social, tended to become a justification and a

---

[11] Anonymous by request.

placeholder for policies that pursued a Hindu-nationalist agenda. As underlying elements of Hindutva surfaced through the language of development 'for all', they increasingly shifted from the fringe extreme-right to the centre of the party. For instance, the Kumbh Mela in 2019 was widely touted as the largest Hindu spiritual gathering in the world, and used to publicise not only India's cultural strength but also India's infrastructural progress and development. The national and the Uttar Pradesh state government administration spent $40 billion and hired a global management consulting firm, Ernst & Young, to manage its large-scale proceedings, offering luxury tents, digital guidance apps, river transport, artificial intelligence crowd control, and almost a thousand special trains (Thacker et al. 2018). The Kumbh Mela effectively sought to make Hindu pride synonymous with Indian national progress.

In a similar vein, the mass arrests, state violence, and black-out of communications in the Muslim-majority area of Kashmir since August 2019 have been justified by the slogan of bringing development to the region, to those who have been long denied it. Sambit Patra, former BJP spokesperson and Lok Sabha candidate in Puri, Orissa, said in a TV interview in April 2019 that 'Hinduism is synonymous with development'. Disruption, here, is understood as bold and decisive policy, where surgical strikes against Pakistan, demonetisation, and the occupation of Kashmir are lauded as necessary for the betterment of domestic politics, security, and economy.

In making Hinduism coexistent with nationhood, the adminis-tration and its supporters have projected Hindutva as a trans-historical, seemingly inclusive bloc, reifying the deep emotional and cognitive appeal they hold. They echo a speech made by Modi in Parliament in 2015, where he responded to allegations by the oppos-ition that the Sangh Parivar is homogeneously Hindu: 'The percep-tions you talk about are very old. BJP isn't an upper caste or Hindi-belt party. BJP is in power in states with high Christian, Sikh and Muslim voters' (India Today 2015). In the process, the BJP has appropriated

nationalist heroes such as Gandhi and Ambedkar to pursue its nationalist rhetoric. For example, Gandhi's iconography is used as the
mouthpiece for one of Modi's flagship campaigns, Swachh Bharat,
which encourages citizens to keep their neighbourhoods and streets
clean. Indeed, the irony of this iconography is that it was a member of
the RSS who assassinated Gandhi in 1948 allegedly for allowing India
to be partitioned and 'unfairly favourable to Muslims' (Patel 2022). The
BJP has also appropriated Ambedkar, a stalwart of Dalit, anti-caste and
anti-discrimination politics, for campaigns to appeal to a wider range of
lower-caste and working-class constituents. The BJP government in
Uttar Pradesh even went as far as to pass a State Assembly resolution
to add 'Ramji', a name alluding to the hero in the Hindu epic
Ramayana, to B. R. Ambedkar's name, henceforth referring to him as
B. R. Ramji Ambedkar (ANI 2018; Upadhyay 2018).[12]

Modi's public persona, charisma, and carefully manufactured
presence on social media have been a source of deep scholarly fascin-
ation, with good reason. Yet it would be a mistake to see the BJP's
phenomena as powered only by a charismatic, larger-than-life leader.
Rather, targeting policy solutions in politically powerful ways
requires the mobilisation of several different tools aimed at unifying
contradictory interests and building, as Stuart Hall (1979) suggests, an
'alternative logic' that works on the basis of already constituted
social practices and lived ideologies, but with altered 'weight of
condensations within any one discourse'. In the Indian case, the
BJP government has used politically resonant discourse to 'sell' its
behaviour through religious and moral imperatives. Here is where

---

[12] This is a particularly ahistorical move considering Ambedkar's legacy of critiquing
both Hinduism and the idea of a Hindu state. He is recorded to have written: 'I shall
have no faith in Rama and Krishna who are believed to be incarnations of God nor
shall I worship them' (Kelkar 2014). Similarly, his works have expressed critique of
all forms of nationhood on the basis of religion, whether it be Hinduism or Islam.
If anything gets in the way of social assimilation between Hindus and Muslims, he
has said, it is Hinduism and Islam (Ambedkar 1941). Ambedkar was also a key
member of the committee in charge of drafting the Indian Constitution, disregarded
by the RSS, which makes these tensions more resonant.

Modi's extraordinary (both in the senses of being of the people and, yet, their ultimate protector) persona plays an integral role in seaming together contradictory narratives. In the words of journalist Pankaj Mishra (2019), Modi has enlivened and 'enriched private lives of fantasy'. The BJP IT cells have worked their way into people's digital worlds through social media, WhatsApp, Twitter, and Facebook, using Modi as a 'maestro of digital psycho-politics' (Mishra 2019) to reconfigure the inner worlds of voters.

Through Modi's personal app (NaMo App), he communicates with his party and supporters; through his publicly broadcast TV channel (the NaMo Channel), the government broadcasted his speeches and a biographical, hagiographic film about his life on repeat. He demonstrates a commitment to Hindu spirituality frequently through appearing on YouTube videos about yoga and religious rituals. In seeking to turn the 'leader into the truth' (Naidu 2016), Modi's public persona blurs boundaries between identifying with him as a public leader, and as a private psychological relief and saviour. In Modi's first few rallies before the 2019 state elections of Uttar Pradesh and Uttarakhand, he claimed that the Congress Party invented the myth of Hindu terror and violence, invoking sentimentality and victimhood in the crowd by asking 'didn't it hurt your feelings?' In another interview with the BJP-supporting TV anchor, Arnab Goswami, Modi claimed that voters had a choice between two ideologies: to accept Hinduism as a sacred, ancient culture, or to malign all Hindus by falsely fabricating the concept of Hindu terror.

The head of strategic studies at a prominent think tank explains how Modi is able to overcome contradictions amongst his party and supporters:

> We [must] acknowledge that the RSS has fundamentally altered the political landscape of this country and therefore you have to counter it from a different vantage point, you can't really use the older frames to counter it. The BJP today is no longer a Hindi heartland, cowbelt party, Modi wouldn't have been elected if it was.

There's an underestimation of the ability of the BJP to expand its wings, and with that comes contradictions because you will never be able to manage the contradictions in a way that allows you a seamless narrative.

I think those contradictions are only going to multiply but as long as they have Modi, they can massage those contradictions because he's a larger than life leader who can manipulate when he goes out on a campaign trail.

(Interview with head of strategic studies at a prominent New Delhi think tank,[13] March 2019)

The spectacle of the Modi persona and the loose 'mental frameworks' (Pankowski 2010) of the BJP's governing ideologies have combined to soothe the contradictions between the party's moderate technocratic language and its polarising political discourse. The administration's first mass attack on left-liberal intellectuals in 2016 marked a key symbolic and moral–cultural move to protect the interests of a unified, Hindu India. The government arrested several activists, protestors, and students, for participating in a mass protest against the government's occupation of Kashmir. Held in the Jawaharlal Nehru University, the protest was nationally derided by the government and the BJP's media sources for hosting 'anti-national' sentiments. As a follow-up, the former Human Resources Development Minister, Smriti Irani, spoke in Parliament calling protestors, activists, and those who expressed dissent, the 'Tukde Tukde Gang'. Literally, the Tukde Tukde Gang translates to 'breaking-up gang', alluding to dissenters as destroying the unity of India. Such political rhetoric is only one example of the many ways the BJP administration and its supporters have scrutinised and stamped out dissent. More recently, the government has frequently used the Unlawful Activities Prevention Act (UAPA) to arrest students, activists, journalists, and authors who publicly critique the government.

[13] Anonymous by request.

Throughout, the economic right coincides with the political, cultural, authoritarian right. Discourses of national economic strength geared towards a protectionist framework are mobilised towards bolstering participation in international trade, global finance, deregulation, and fewer labour protections, and presented as being towards 'development for all', to protect India's interests and build India's prominence on the global stage. To use Desai's (2016) term, there is a 'danse macabre' of the two, that is, a hybridised discourse and practice. The effort is viewed as a profoundly moral endeavour to protect the integrity and identity of India – an India where the collective 'we' is coded as indigenously Hindu, and proud. Rhetoric that may have previously been mobilised to support a protectionist and self-reliant economy is re-contextualized to support and bolster further global participation. Indeed, discourses of economic nationalism can be compatible with a wide range of policy orientations (Helleiner 2021). In the next section, I show how the ruling administration has channelled hypernationalist popular discontent to enact neoliberal economic policies.

'Cleaning Up' the Economy

State interventionism has long been a core emphasis of Indian postcolonial nationalism across party lines, yet the liberalisation of the Indian economy in 1991 gave way to new orientations of public and private participation. In order to trace shifts in dominant economic discourse since Independence, I offer a brief chronological summary of the BJP–RSS's policy movements. Through this section, I show how the BJP–RSS's economic and social policies are linked and dependent on one another, and historically predicated on building a Hindu social identity (Palshikar 2015).

Championing Economic Nationalism (1980s): Between 1947 and the 1990s, political proponents of Hindu nationalism placed a significant emphasis on the collective society over the individual and over the state. Yet, for the most part, this constituency considered state intervention a necessary tool to protect people from the vagaries of the market. Upon Upadhyaya's death, Atal Bihari Vajpayee became the leader of the Jana Sangh that later became the Bharatiya Janata Party, the BJP, in 1980. Vajpayee emphasised a focus on social and economic policy to lead the party to gain more traction nationally (Chacko 2018), and recruited several high-profile leaders without Hindu-nationalist backgrounds. At this time, the BJP positioned itself in opposition to the Congress Party's pro-business policy turn and emphasised *swadeshi* (self-reliance), decentralisation, grassroots welfare activities, small-scale industry, and rural communities, with only subtle undercurrents of Hindu nationalism.

When the BJP lost the 1984 national election to Rajiv Gandhi of the Congress Party, the RSS regained control over the party and reinstituted its core focus on Hindu nationalism. Rajiv Gandhi, colloquially known as 'Mr. Clean', for having kept a distance from 'political dirt', saw himself as a political outsider who was able to bring in a 'new style of functioning' (Agrawal and Sharma 1993). He assembled a think tank–like set-up at his personal office (Kidwai 2010), which included technocrats and corporate professionals who were all relatively privileged, cosmopolitan, and educated at elite institutions. The 1980s saw the liberalisation of the telecommunication industry in India and the advent of technological modernisation. As such, Rajiv Gandhi's new style of functioning relied on the valorisation of data, an emphasis on technology, and the skills offered by business-like technocrats and white-collared professionals (Sharma 2022). Yet, despite wider expansions in computers and technology, his attempt to instil rigorous tech-based data analytics as a tool for political and policy processes did not gain widespread traction until long after his tenure (see details in Chapter 4).

At the same time, the Vishwa Hindu Parishad (VHP), an arm of the Sangh Parivar, adopted a resolution demanding the 'liberation' of the Babri Masjid, declaring it to be Lord Ram's birthplace. In 1986, L. K. Advani took over as president of the BJP and catalysed the Ram Janmabhoomi Mandir movement: a campaign that sought to build a temple honouring Lord Ram's birthplace in Ayodhya, over the precise location where sixteenth-century mosque called the Babri Masjid currently stood.

Mandir, Mandal, and Intra-Party Expansion (1990–1999): The 1989 election offered the BJP the opportunity to consolidate Hindu votes by entering into a partnership with the National Front (a block of state and regional parties opposed to the Congress Party) and successfully supporting V. P. Singh in his bid for prime ministership. The BJP also solidified its identity as a Hindu majoritarian party by vitriolically campaigning nationwide for the demolition of the Babri Masjid, claiming that it was originally the birthplace of Lord Ram. In 1990, Advani led a *rath yatra* (a chariot journey) with thousands of volunteers from the Sangh Parivar across hundreds of towns and villages in India on his way to Ayodhya (Ghassem-Fachandi 2012). Advani held approximately six rallies a day and sparked many anti-Muslim riots in his wake. On V. P. Singh's order, the chief minister of the Bihar government arrested Advani as he passed through the state, leading the BJP to withdraw support from V. P. Singh's government and causing his support base to collapse.[14] The BJP used its role in the Ram Mandir movement as a central appeal in the 1991 parliamentary elections, doubling its percentage of votes nationwide and becoming the second largest party in the Lok Sabha (Lower House of the Parliament).

The 1991 national elections also coincided with Rajiv Gandhi's assassination. While no party was able to win an overall majority in the Lok Sabha, the Congress Party won more seats than any other party and formed a minority government. In response to the burgeoning economic crisis spurred by an account deficit, declining investor confidence, and currency overvaluation, the Congress Party sought economic bailout from the IMF and, as a condition, introduced economic reforms and liberalised the national economy (some note by

---

[14] V. P. Singh's government was followed by another short-lived government led by Chandrashekhar, a smaller faction of the Janata Dal with outside support from the Congress Party.

'stealth') in 1991 (Jenkins 2003). Political analysts and economists at both ends of the political spectrum have noted that paradigms governing economic policy have continued on a similar path since the 1991 economic reforms, throughout successive BJP and Congress government administrations (Chhibber and Verma 2018; Kohli 2009).

During the 1990s, the BJP unified its heterogeneous support base by lending support to lower-middle-class disaffected Hindu youth, often upper caste or middle caste, who feared economic precarity and opposed caste-based and Muslim affirmative action policies. In November 1992, the Supreme Court upheld the Mandal Commission's controversial decision to grant caste-based affirmative action (reservations) for government jobs to OBCs (Other Backward Classes). This move led to large-scale agitation from the BJP. Soon after, the BJP, RSS, and VHP marched to demolish the Babri Masjid. Following the destruction of the Babri Masjid in 1992, vitriol and inhuman brutality against Muslims washed over the country. The then prime minister, P. V. Narasimha Rao, temporarily banned the RSS (Rattanani 2020), yet they remained undeterred. From the 1990s onwards, the BJP oscillated between favouring the market as a catalyst for political and economic growth, while pressure from the RSS enforced its support of state protection in industry and agriculture and the Ram Mandir movement solidified its strong Hindu identity (Chacko 2019; Dhattiwala and Biggs 2012; Jaffrelot 2007).

Despite internal opposition from more orthodox elements in the party, Govindacharya (who was then a general secretary of the BJP) advocated for allowing OBC political aspirants more space within the party (Palshikar 2015). Throughout the 1990s, the rank and file in the party became more accommodating of Dalits, Scheduled Tribes, and OBCs (Thachil 2014), which eventually changed the composition of BJP's elected representatives (Hansen and Jaffrelot 1998). During this period, the BJP also gained support from middle-class Hindus who had benefited from the economic reforms, but were growing resentful of the Congress Party's redistributive welfare programmes, caste-based affirmative action, and rumoured corruption (Chacko 2018).

Coalition-Building, Globalisation and Gujarat Pogrom (1999–2004): The BJP briefly held power in 1996 and then in 1998 but their governments were short-lived, collapsing due to shifting coalitions and hung parliaments. In 1999, the BJP-led coalition, called the National Democratic Alliance (NDA), won the national elections: the first time since 1984 that a party had won with an outright majority and the first time a non-Congress prime minister would serve a full five-year term. By the early 2000s, Vajpayee had shifted from advocating for state protection of small-scale markets and a 'calibrated globalisation' (Chacko 2019, 393), to pushing the state to make small and medium enterprises more globally competitive, supporting public–private partnerships (known as Special Economic Zones), lifting import restrictions in agricultural and textile markets, and self-employment (Chacko 2019). During the latter half of the 1990s and the early 2000s, the BJP worked to build its support base and, in trying to build coalitions with other parties, moderated some of its more contentious viewpoints (such as the Ram Janmabhoomi movement, the abrogation of Article 370, and a uniform civil code).

In 2002, Narendra Modi who was then the chief minister of Gujarat, presided over a violent anti-Muslim pogrom across the state, which led to the brutal rape and murder of thousands of Muslim men, women, and children. The pogrom was seemingly in response to a train fire that killed fifty-eight Hindu pilgrims returning from Ayodhya. Yet the retaliation against Muslims has been considered by rights organisations and political opposition to be a state-directed form of ethnic cleansing, as Modi, the police force, and state officials have been accused of directing rioters and handing out lists of Muslim-owned properties (Jackson et al. 2011). Modi's tenure as chief minister, however, ushered in unprecedented growth and business development in Gujarat, which served to whitewash his alleged involvement in the riots (Sud 2022).

The BJP's 2004 'India Shining' re-election campaign sought to ride on the wave of market-based development policy, targeting urban middle- and upper-class Indians as investor-consumer citizens who reaped the rewards of liberalisation (Chacko 2018; Kaur 2016). Despite Vajpayee's popularity, the BJP coalition lost the 2004 elections. The uneven experience of liberalisation, particularly that of a large majority who were excluded from the apparent benefits and faced rising inequality, job loss, and livelihood insecurity, led to the BJP's election loss. The Congress Party won using a slogan proclaiming 'Aam aadmi ko kya mila? [What did the common man get?]'. Indeed, urban-, rural-, upper-, middle-, and lower-class Indians may have disapproved of disinvestment and foreign investment, which represented a larger crisis of legitimacy for market-based development policies and sapped the BJP's core support base (Chhibber and Verma 2018; Mukherji 2013). The Congress Party, in turn, capitalised on this dissatisfaction and promised inclusive growth, 'freedom from hunger and unemployment', and introduced a new era of political incorporation for the neoliberal era (Chacko 2018). This involved rewriting the informal, unorganised economy, which existed outside of labour regulations, protections, and industrial zones, as 'a dynamic site of entrepreneurship and innovation', casting the 'entrepreneurial poor' (Irani 2019, 40) as producer and agent.

Fighting Corruption and 'Policy Paralysis' (2004–2014): The Congress Party's coalition won successive elections and ruled from 2004 to 2014, proffering 'inclusive growth' – a policy framework that aimed to mitigate the effects of the World Bank's recommended pro-market reforms through providing some safety nets. They thus attempted to address resulting inequalities and a growing precariat with a range of social and secular welfare programmes and rights-based legislation, including the National Rural Employment Guarantee Act, Right to Fair Compensation, Transparency in Land Acquisition, Rehabilitation and Resettlement Act (LARR), Right to Food Act, and

Right to Information Act. Despite these attempts at redistributive policies and the recommendations of a range of activists, experts, and civil society groups, the Congress administration struggled internally with a lack of consensus on issues that reflected different understandings of accountability and transparency. The National Advisory Council, made up of activists, intellectuals, and left-liberal academics and convened by the Congress Party president, urged the prime minister to understand that rising inequality and jobless growth was a result of structural factors and market failure. In a particular discussion about the problems of the Public Distribution System for subsidised food grain, for example, the Right to Food campaigners interpreted the problems as a result of an overbearing technocratic regulatory system and market failure. Yet Prime Minister Manmohan Singh and the Parliamentary Standing Committee instead saw the need for further efficiency and a reliance on the market, through direct cash transfers, procurement caps, and per capita entitlements (Chacko 2018).

Several NAC members quit the Council during the Congress Party's second tenure (2009–2014), during which the government legislated to restrict foreign funding to civil society groups and NGOs as a way to stem organised resistance to government projects in mining, GMFs, and nuclear energy. The Congress administration's overwhelming tendency was less to democratise policymaking and more to isolate it within highly technocratic and top-down, depoliticised forms of governance (Chacko 2018). This came to be perceived as a blindness to the needs of the 'people', an impression which was bolstered by a series of high-profile corruption scandals revealing Congress politicians and government officials to be using regulatory mechanisms to syphon off money for themselves. As the Congress faced a 'crisis of legitimacy' (Chacko 2018) and became increasingly risk-averse to passing legislation, the BJP and the opposition used this opportunity to disrupt parliamentary proceedings, resulting in an overwhelming narrative of the government's 'policy paralysis'.

In 2011, social activist Anna Hazare led mass protests and a popular India Against Corruption movement funded by corporate leaders and receiving core support from the middle and upper classes.[15] This anti-corruption mobilisation was eventually adopted by the BJP, RSS, and other Hindu-nationalist groups. Leading up to the 2014 elections, the BJP abandoned its older, national leadership in favour of a younger leader, Modi, who was able to build a strong opposition built on promises of transparency, accountability, and decentralisation coupled with a history of Hindutva allegiance.

Citizen as Stakeholder, Entrepreneur, and Hindu (2014–Present): I contend that from 2014, the BJP began to strategically combine anti-corruption and welfare-based discourse with neoliberal reforms and national security in a distinct fashion. Rather than using the language of 'inclusive growth' as the Congress Party before it had done, it placed heavy emphasis on developing a digitised welfare architecture (Chacko 2018). This made significant appeals to an aspirational public through promoting 'entrepreneurial citizenship' (Irani 2019) while promising to dismantle caste-based affirmative action and deliver a range of targeted welfare services. At the same time, the BJP has been expanding its social base beyond middle- to upper-caste constituents, to rural areas and amongst lower caste, tribal, and underrepresented groups. During the 2014 and 2019 election campaigns, party workers were able to target several 'last mile' villages in the Northern belt, where no other political party workers were present (Chhibber and Verma 2014). Of course, as Irani (2019) and Sanyal (2007) have noted, the digitisation of welfare and managing the 'need economy' (Sanyal 2007) through delivering state entitlements or encouraging social enterprise (Roy 2010) has long been the domain of programmes funded by NGOs, aid organisations, and philanthropies. This particular discourse, as I will elaborate, differs in that citizens, particularly the disenfranchised, are not only

---

[15] For an analysis of the 2011 anti-corruption movement and Anna Hazare's political demands and fault lines, see Hansen (2008) and Chacko (2018).

producers and consumers: the state offers them the opportunity to be *stakeholders* in their own future.

Parallel to these promises, the BJP's successful 2019 election campaign thrived on unstable national security, where national fantasies encouraged by the administration became ones of fear, protection, nationalist boundaries, and aggression. In Modi's victory speech, he said, 'This is a victory for self-respect. This election has given self-respect a new face. There used to be a mask called secularism. In this election, not even one seat was fought from secularism ... people have not had the *himmat* [guts] to say the word over the last five years' (translated from televised speech, May 2019). Here, Modi seems to be drawing a distinction between 'fake' secularism, which he says has been practised since Independence through appeasing Muslims and minorities; and 'true' secularism, which, according to him, allows for (economic) 'empowerment' of minorities rather than a re-enforcement of their victimhood and minority status. This demonstrates how the conversations and terms of national debate had shifted dramatically in the last five years, allowing the prime minister to erase a key feature of the constitution in his victory speech. The latter interpretation of secularism speaks to what Reddy (2018) identifies as a duality of neo-Hindutva: a force that projects aggressive majoritarianism, while simultaneously claiming an anti-political 'neutral' face of inter-religious inclusion.

In an interview with Swapan Dasgupta, a former BJP Member of Parliament, journalist, and public intellectual, I asked how internal conversations within the party negotiated economic policy and Hindu majoritarianism. Considering the many factions of opposing economic ideologies within the party, the RSS, and their supporters, he said:

SD: In 1991, when liberalisation came into force, the BJP was confronted with this choice of, you know, what do we do, do we support this, etc. There were views on both sides, interesting ideas, and there was an interesting debate. And I think, at one time, Advani [senior leader of the BJP] clinched the issue, as far as I can remember ... I think he opened my eyes to this thing, when he said sort of casually – 'but of course we will never fight elections on economic issues'.

Researcher: Oh wow, and what did he mean?

SD: He meant that, you know, why should we bring up all these issues and create tensions within the party? There is an overall agreement on one set of things, let's fight it on that.

Researcher: So the tensions with an economic policy, protectionist or globalist, that's what you're referring to.

SD: There are so many – that's one way of putting it. But you know, whether you emphasise the organised or unorganised sector – and there are strong voices on both sides. But what unites them at the end of the day, it's [the party's] commitment to that social identity.

Here, Dasgupta acknowledges that the fluidity of the BJP's economic ideology is predicated on its otherwise unifying Hindutva claims to nationhood. He affirms that regardless of contradictions and opposing economic ideologies, the BJP is able to consolidate a support base through its commitment to a Hindu national identity. A contesting BJP MP told me in March 2019, 'Why are we muddled in our way of economy? Because we haven't thought through very clearly what economic model we want for India. We have done very well on the social side, the [RSS]. That's why we are today the largest NGO.'

Leading up to the 2014 election, the party maintained a strong undercurrent of Hindu nationalism by sometimes articulating its economic policy through idioms of Hindu civilisational supremacy, and at other times presenting a technocratic and centrist legitimacy. The BJP's policy priorities in the 2014 election campaign then were in direct response to the Congress government's corruption scams and a concurrent economic slowdown between 2009 and 2014. Modi's appeal as the BJP's prime ministerial candidate was based in combining both cultural and economic nationalist ideologies: the former through his presiding over the anti-Muslim pogrom in Gujarat during his chief ministerial tenure in 2002, and the latter through his role as modernising administrator in turning Gujarat into a centre for business investment. Despite his building strong relationships with industrialists and promising a range of business-friendly economic reforms, deregulation, and labour reforms, the party still positioned Modi as a spokesperson for the 'people' against corporate corruption. This inconsistent discourse fixed what was lacking in the party's previous administration's appeal.

Between 1999 and 2004, the BJP's coalition government attempted to pursue market-centric policies by selling twelve public sector companies, but this did not politically resonate with either their working class or their business class constituents. As Dhiraj Nayyar, the former head of Economics at NITI Aayog (the government's primary internal think tank) notes, 'there is no great constituency for market reform'. According to Nayyar, Modi is seen to have spurred on a paradigm shift: for citizens to become 'stakeholders', thus encouraging a behavioural change.

> Modi's skill was that he was able to understand what was agitating the people ... and that formed the policy priority. I think he's done exactly what his priorities were, and his priority was never to be a Reagan or Thatcher or something. It was basically to first of all, clean up the system, because he was elected to clean up the system. Look at the policies that were completed. If you look at demonetisation, the goods and services tax, bankruptcy law (which is the first time businessmen are losing control of their businesses, if they're run to the ground), and the real estate 'benami' properties act.
>
> These four-five big reforms which have been pushed through are basically following exactly that promised 'cleanliness', the cleaning

up of the economy. That's one side of it. The second is that we're gonna make the government deliver to the people, using technology to deliver direct benefits, insurance schemes, and the Jan Dhan accounts. It was a mix of cleaning up the mess and, to some extent, getting the government's act together in terms of delivering better services for the poor.

(Interview with Dhiraj Nayyar, former head of Economics at NITI Aayog, May 2019)

As Nayyar claims, the campaign's discourse was to 'correct' the government, rather than to dismantle it and unleash the market. While historically, dominant Indian political discourse has often promised redistribution, Modi's administration has largely dismantled redistributive policy paradigms. Between 2014–2019, the BJP government cut social welfare policy spending with a major decline in funds given to NREGA, Right to Food, and other major programmes. Ram Madhav (former National General Secretary, BJP) proudly spoke of this, saying that the BJP in power has meant that:

We no longer see people of this country as just voters, nor just as citizens. Now, policy-level thinking is that they have to be stakeholders. Progressive programs have to be developed in such a way that they become stakeholders – not just beneficiaries, not just citizens. So that's why if you take Swachh Bharat, if you take Stand-Up India, Innovate India, Skill India, in these, they are stakeholders. That is a very important shift we have brought in. Secondly, we have decided that the government should not do everything.

The PM's slogan has been 'minimum government but maximum governance', so the government should be a facilitator, not just a beneficiary. We now allow people to access government benefits, but stand on their own feet. They don't have anything to do with the government. I give you one million Indian rupees, take it from me, but stand on your own feet, don't look up to me for jobs. So a job seeker can also become a job creator. But here the approach is that the government is only there to facilitate, not everything the government can take care of.

(Interview with Ram Madhav, former National General Secretary of BJP, February 2019)

Shifting the delivery of basic goods and services to the private sector is a politically sensitive move for a country with a welfarist history (Kohli 2009, 2012). Indeed, foundational thinkers within the RSS and the BJP, such as Golwalkar and Upadhyaya, historically advocated for the state to maintain responsibility for core public goods, such as health and education. The BJP has messaged these shifts strategically, tapping into resonant feelings of state patronage, individual empowerment, and aspirational entrepreneurship. Even as they escalate the privatisation of public goods, their rhetoric sells their policies as an increase in state welfare and paternalism. Indeed, the fact that a sputtering economy and severe unemployment (Vaishnav 2019) did not diminish Modi's grand election victory in 2019 marks the importance of his narrative and the speculative trust (what Sircar (2020) calls 'vishwas politics') that a majority of the citizenship places in his government.

This messaging has morphed over the government's five-year tenure between 2014 and 2019: at first, it was delivered entirely as a stakeholder-centric set of schemes, promising citizen empowerment and 'minimum governance'. Then, when facing state election losses in Delhi and Bihar, and accusations of crony capitalism by the opposition that Modi's BJP was a 'suit boot ki sarkaar' (government of the suited-booted corporate), this shifted to a more state-centric messaging of 'patronage plus efficiency', as the party wanted to avoid giving the impression that they were making business-friendly policy. The anti-incumbency sentiment against the Congress Party in the 2014 national election was on the basis of opposing self-interested political corruption, insulated technocratic control, and bureaucratic state stagnation – all of which are targeted by this discursive combination of citizen stakeholder plus state efficiency.

Thus, previous social welfare policies have been replaced by Innovate India, Stand-Up India, and Skill India (a number of entrepreneurial programmes), while demands for better healthcare have resulted in the Ayushman Bharat scheme, a health insurance programme to incentivize the building of private hospitals in rural areas. In turn, this allows the private sector to participate in the delivery of each of these goods while the state messages them through a narrative of semi-patronage. With Start-Up India, Modi's government promises to allow a new generation of entrepreneurs to thrive. As Nayyar notes, 'the government always intended for people to have their own stake and money in a particular scheme ... Modi wants to get the private guys in, the government in, and the stakeholder-citizen has to put in some monetary contribution' (interview with Nayyar, May 2019).

The discourse of corruption shaped a large part of the messaging surrounding the 'cleaning up' of the economy. Examining the strategic use of this discourse (Gupta 1995) allows us to understand the relationship of the state to social groups on two registers: first, it enables people to construct the state symbolically; and second, it allows them to define themselves as citizens who are continuously affected by and invested in the state. By fluctuating between corruption and accountability, the state presents itself as nurturing and paternalistic, yet simultaneously 'fixing' itself from within and attacking both corrupt politicians and market actors. At the same time, an anti-corruption discourse can also be an exemplary form of shifting responsibility away from middle classes and private corporations and blaming politicians and the government for being the sole 'bad actors'. The anti-corruption Lokpal movement in 2011 'externalised corruption into the domain of politics and absolved the middle classes of all comparable culpability' (Reddy 2018, 4) – thus becoming the domain of anti-politics. In the next section, I show how the government's demonetisation move in 2016 can serve as a representative event of how ideas of accountability, transparency, and protection seep into the realm of national identity and symbolic justification.

Demonetisation as a Case Study

Demonetisation had several shifting goalposts. On 8 November 2016, Prime Minister Narendra Modi stated all ₹500 and ₹1,000 notes (the highest denominations) would lose monetary value in a few hours to curb 'black money'. This dictated limited time periods of when and how much money could be exchanged for new notes, and how much money could be withdrawn from ATMs. These decrees changed frequently. From dismantling black money to curbing terrorist funds, to moving towards a cashless economy and improving interest rates, the professed aims of the government's (or, rather, Modi's) constantly changing decrees had powerful effects on the moral strength of the move. Regardless, it was constructed as necessary, from an attack on black money to a move towards a 'cashless economy'.

The rhetoric justifying demonetisation was soon moulded into a larger path towards 'transforming' India through symbolic nationalism. In the public presentation of demonetisation, such as Modi's public speeches and newspaper articles written by members of the BJP, particular iterations of market freedom (or regulation) were aligned with symbols of pro-poor nationalism and self-sacrifice. While demonetisation, digital banking, cash transfers, and the BJP's other financial flagship programmes appear to want to build a market-investor-consumer citizen, the BJP's ideal citizens are also tied up in distinctive forms of cultural, Indian, and Hindu pride. Indeed, Modi's authoritarian leadership style complemented the decision-oriented nature of this policy move in a way that connected and relieved a spectrum of anxieties.

An opinion piece written by M. Venkaiah Naidu, the former president of the BJP and former vice president of India, justified demonetisation as the path towards not only a new era but also a particular kind of era that has purged the degeneration of its past:

> Let us examine demonetisation in the overall context of our institutional culture that has evolved since Independence. There may not be too many dissenting voices if I say that the prime

contours of the existing decadent culture are corruption, opportunism, nepotism, greed, repression (remember Emergency?), exploitation of power, sycophancy and self-seeking behaviour. Non-Congress governments made sincere efforts to change this culture but the results fell short given their too brief interregnums. So, everyone knows which party is primarily responsible for this entrenched decadent culture.

(Naidu 2016)

Modi, too, refers to this history of decadence as an 'epidemic':

Brother and sisters this is a 70 year old epidemic that I need to wipe out in 17 months. I tell you, only I know, I am looting their 70 year corrupt earnings. I am aware they may not let me live.

(PTI 2016)

There is, here, a strategic interaction of existing discourses. Modi and Naidu are echoing a rhetoric of post-Independence, anti-colonial nationalism, while blaming the Congress Party's seventy-year legacy for continuing the elite excesses of colonial rule. In other moments, Modi has consciously appropriated the Congress Party's narratives and Gandhian imagery, both in policy propaganda as well as spiritually sentimental speeches to appeal to his audiences. On Gandhi's birthday in 2017, he tweeted saying, 'Gandhi Ji made this world a better place. His ideals, dedication to the poor & struggle against injustice inspire'. At other moments, Modi has made explicit efforts to draw parallels between himself and Gandhi – accentuating their common roots in Gujarat, taking Gandhi's historic train journey in South Africa[16] that inspired him to fight racial discrimination in the country, and using his image as the icon for his 'Swachh Bharat (Clean India)' campaign. His rhetoric not only forces parallels between him and Gandhi but also strategically transfers a whitewashed mass nostalgia for Gandhi's

---

[16] The Prime Minister's Office Twitter account reported: 'PM travels from Pentrich Railway Station to Pietermaritzburg. Train resembles the one on which Gandhi ji travelled.'

legacy to Modi's leadership and personhood, adopting Hindu-ised icon-ography of Gandhi towards national development.

While echoing and leveraging these discourses to their benefit, Modi and Naidu are also, importantly, rejecting them. Despite strategic-ally using the rhetoric of these narratives, they are recontextualising them by deeming the last seventy years of post-Independence rule an 'old, decadent culture' of India. In the 1980s, the Congress Party's prime minister, Rajiv Gandhi, held a belief in the possibility of technology to clean up the economy, address inefficiency, and fix corrupt power-brokering amongst political classes. Yet Modi and the BJP build narra-tives that erase this history, making only themselves synonymous with technological efficiency, transparency, and righteousness.

This history of persecution ties into a much longer, existing story of right-wing Hindu victimisation – something that is built into Modi's actions, words, and politics, both implicitly and explicitly. This narrative begins by arguing that India was a Hindu civilisation that has been invaded for centuries: first by the Mughals (the Muslim rulers), then the British, and, after Independence, by the decadent and secular Congress government. The Congress government is accused of not only determining politics but also the construction of the nation in its social, cultural, and political history.

The 'cult of the leader' element, as I mentioned earlier, is clear in demonetisation's roll-out. Indeed, it is present in most of Modi's propaganda and the administration's mass advertising. Modi's image dominates the majority of posters, briefs, and letters assuring people of the nurturing state, prefacing the consequential decisions he made with an ease that was denied to previous leaders and parties. In many ways, the cult-like status of the leader enables him to deploy seem-ingly contradictory political strategies (both populist and techno-cratic) because he somehow embodies a 'national soul' (Bhatt 2001). The following excerpts from his speech more concisely demonstrate the extent to which his bodily form has come to stand in for several components of the moral self: a servant of the masses and a self-sacrificing leader for the good of the people:

Now, you tell me dear brothers and sisters, didn't you vote me into power to fight against corruption? Didn't you choose me to curb black money? At that time you also knew that if I act against these menaces you would face some problems. Didn't you know? All knew there would be hardships.

Brothers and sisters, I was not born to capture power. My dear countrymen, I have left my home, my family, everything for the nation. Some do it out of pressure. A large number of my countrymen want to be honest.

I had very clearly stated on 8th November in my address that you must be ready to face the hardships. I am witnessing thousands of countrymen standing in queues for saving their country.

(Firstpost 2016)

Modi constructs a mythology of his own hardship and self-sacrifice. His promise of rooting out corruption justifies how his policy disciplined the country's citizens into self-sacrifice in exchange for the 'greater good' that remains unclear. The 'decisionism' (Pandian and Roy 2014) of Modi's authoritarian leadership style falls into providing moral certainty throughout these supposedly temporary inconveniences, creating a spectrum of deferred justice and shared ideology for all. In a national newspaper, Venkaiah Naidu has referred to this leader-driven moral certainty as a 'new cultural revolution' (Naidu 2016) in the lineage of Mao Zedong. Naidu's piece goes on to say:

Targeted behavioural modification will eventually result in the elimination of black money leading to increased revenues to Central and state governments that ultimately benefits the poor, common man and the middle classes. Finally, the new initiatives will soon transform India, erasing the legacy of the old decadent culture and Modi will emerge as the tallest leader of post-Independence India.

(Naidu 2016)

Naidu's declaration that Modi will emerge as the tallest leader of post-Independence India exemplifies Modi's strategic personalisation. The idea for demonetisation was seemingly suggested to Modi by Anil Bokil, founder of a think tank in Pune called ArthaKranti Pratishthan (Mohan 2016). Yet the secrecy surrounding Modi's announcement, where only a handful of his closest confidants were informed of his decision prior to the national announcement, reinforced his myth as a singular, solitary man who makes the difficult yet necessary decisions. As is evident from the aforementioned speech excerpts, he emphasises his rags-to-riches story and distance from establishment elites, activating 'convincing performances of ordinariness and outsiderness' (Moffitt 2016).

CONCLUSION

Populist resentment against the powerful Indian elite is not without cause. The upper echelons of Indian politics and policymaking have long been composed of close-knit and insular upper-caste and upper-class networks. According to a national population data analysis by Bharti (2018), only 22.28 per cent of the overall population is upper caste (including Brahmin, Rajput, and Bania castes), yet they own 41 per cent of the wealth in the country.[17] The cultural and institutional domination by upper castes is even more extreme (Guru and Sarukkai 2018): a study of caste-based distribution of corporate board members in 2010 indicates that 92.6 per cent of total positions were occupied by upper castes, while OBCs (Other Backward Classes) and SC/STs (Scheduled Castes/Scheduled Tribes) (administrative categories for Dalits and tribals) occupied 3.8 per cent and 3.5 per cent, respectively (Ajit, Donker, and Saxena 2012; Yengde 2019). Even in

---

[17] According to Bharti (2018), the most important and unique factor 'which provides sturdiness to the caste system is the fact that it assigns relative position to every caste in the society. Even though Rajputs come second in hierarchy, they are above 90% of the population. Similarly Banias derive utility by being higher in status to 88% of the population. And this way the caste system has created a situation where all the castes (except the ones at the bottom) derive some kind of superior social status compared to other castes' (Bharti 2018, 10).

higher bureaucratic corridors, only 9 per cent of officers holding the rank of Joint Secretary and above come from OBCs, SC, and ST communities (Dhingra 2018).

Yet, instead of democratising institutions of power and knowledge-making by including more marginalised communities or new avenues for democratic participation, the recent anti-elite mobilisation has seen the resurgence of upper-caste assertion, driven by resentment of the rise of the backward classes (Verniers and Jaffrelot 2020). As Gudavarthy (2018) notes, the movement against the 'other' is sometimes in opposition to economic elites, at other times to Muslims, and at other times to sociocultural elites. Overall, it serves to build a commonality amongst 'cultural subalterns' by appealing to anxieties of declining social power among dominant castes on one hand, and desire for mobility among Dalits and OBCs on the other (Gudavarthy 2018). Since caste groups are unevenly placed across economic, political, and social demographics, the BJP's appeals often reframe conflicting desires across caste and class groups, softening contradictions along a sense of shared national identity. A vitriolic Hindu resurgence has brought about a New Elite, which might often have a similar amount of wealth and education, yet is resentful of being culturally marginalised: 'underpinning the appeal [of Hindu resurgence] is a desire to reclaim the right to speak as the rightful representatives of the country' (Desai 2019). As I discuss in Chapter 3, this New Elite has the economic and social capital to discredit the existing elite, replacing 'consensus' intellectuals (Gudavarthy 2018) with upper-caste Hindus who see themselves as authentically Indian.

3 Replacing the Custodians of Discourse

During its time in power, the BJP has sought to reframe public attitudes to left-liberal intellectuals. When Modi unexpectedly announced his unilateral decision to demonetise the highest denominations of Indian currency in 2016, Nobel Laureate and Professor of Economics Amartya Sen denounced it as a 'despotic action that has struck at the root of an economy based on trust'. In response, Modi said, 'On the one hand are those [critics] who talk of what people at Harvard say, and on the other is a poor man's son, who through his hard work, is trying to improve the economy ... In fact, hard work is much more powerful than Harvard' (PTI 2017). Perhaps one of Modi's catchiest and well-remembered phrases, 'Harvard vs. Hard Work' is only one example of a growing distaste for established intellectuals, liberals, and critics of the BJP government. It is symptomatic of a multi-pronged approach to unseat economic and cultural elites in favour of building a commonality for 'cultural subalterns' (Gudavarthy 2018).

Along with Modi's charismatic leadership, the BJP's rule has given rise to a new common sense legitimised by a growing Hindutva intelligentsia. In the following excerpt from a national newspaper, Swapan Dasgupta, a staunch conservative intellectual and former Member of Parliament, scathingly mocks the 'progressive intelligentsia' accusing Narendra Modi of authoritarianism. Drawing a clear binary between the pedigreed intellectuals of the university elite and 'raw', spirited voices of the 'people', he celebrates the empowered intellectual leadership of new Alt Right[1] thought.

---

[1] The term 'alt-right' was coined by Richard Spencer, a leader of the American white supremacist movement, to refer to an alternative right-wing movement comprised of

A section of the progressive intelligentsia and activist media have created an impression – not least among Indian students and academics in campuses overseas – that India is sliding towards authoritarian rule.

First, this government has made no attempts to co-opt 'public intellectuals' into the power structure, as was the practice during Congress rule. Modi has focused single-mindedly on his mission of transformation without bothering about campus and press club angst. In effect, he has ended their role as arbiters of thought. Finally, the advent of Modi has coincided with the creation of an Alt Right that, while lacking in pedigreed upbringing and academic respectability, has spiritedly challenged the hegemony of the progressives, quite independent of state patronage. Ponderous intellectualism has been met with raw passion. With their exalted status in jeopardy, the erstwhile custodians of discourse have fallen back on the oldest trick in the trade: scream 'fascism'.

(Dasgupta 2018)

Here, Dasgupta is characterising what he understands to be a new 'Alt Right' as a counter-hegemonic mass of previously disenfranchised supporters of Modi. He is not entirely mistaken. In the mid-1990s, 45 per cent of BJP voters were upper caste, 35 per cent were Other Backward Classes (OBC), and merely 20 per cent constituted Scheduled Castes (SC) and Scheduled Tribes (ST). In 2014, the BJP's base grew to include 44 per cent OBCs, 31 per cent from upper castes, and a full 25 per cent SCs and STs (Suri and Verma 2017; Verma 2019, 35). As a recent plethora of scholarship indicates, BJP supporters from villages, small towns, and urban centres across caste and class barriers have found new forms of community both in person and through

anti-establishment politics that centres itself on white superiority and rejects egalitarianism and universalism (Southern Poverty Law Center n.d.). Similar to white nationalism, Hindu nationalism's version of the alt-right argues that Hinduism as an identity, practice, and national foundation is under attack by multicultural forces.

social media. A rise in what Udupa (2018a) calls 'enterprise Hindus' and Chaturvedi (2016), less generously, describes as 'internet trolls' indicates that these young Indians find a sense of offline belonging and community through engaging in extreme Hindutva rhetoric online.

Dasgupta's contention that the 'raw passion' of the new right lacks pedigree, however, is not accurate. They do, in many cases, claim academic respectability, high stature in bureaucratic or military services, corporate or civil society experience and expertise, or political influence. While the BJP attracted a greater share of OBC, SC, and ST voters in 2014 than it had in previous elections, the BJP's parliamentary ranks are overwhelmingly upper caste, with two out of three cabinet ministers being from upper-caste communities (Suri and Verma 2017). Dasgupta, for example, was a research fellow at Oxford University, and a prominent journalist. Regardless, Dasgupta's declaration of this sociopolitical change symbolises a clear break in the status quo of how expertise is treated and understood. On the one hand, this moment can be characterised as anti-intellectual. Over the last five years, the Indian right wing has been discrediting left-liberal academics and experts, and encouraging pseudo-scientific religious knowledge systems. Yet the Alt Right has also been forging its *own* institutional networks of anointed intellectuals and experts: an ostensibly anti-colonial alternative authority to challenge the 'hegemony of the progressives' and the 'erstwhile custodians of discourse'. So, while they are discrediting an existing group of left-liberal intellectuals for being elite, they are also producing their own intellectual elite.

This chapter examines the evolution of a shifting network of experts and elites who have worked to bring legitimacy to a varied set of policy imperatives within political discourse. Through a study of Indian think tanks, I show how Modi's government combines populist mobilisation with new forms of technocratic expertise to produce a distinct form of nationalist rhetoric. Such a study of policy organisations can explain how they influence dominant policy debates, enable particular classifications of target groups, and legitimise policy solutions while marginalising others (Wedel et al. 2005). I argue that two primary forms of political legitimacy have emerged in contemporary India: (1) *populist politics*, which appeals to the masses/majority by defining nationalism through rigid boundaries of caste, class, and religion; and (2) *technocratic policy*, which produces a consensus of pragmatism and neutralises charges of hyper-nationalism.[2] There is a strong relational dynamic between the two: they function through different, often contradictory, logics and content, yet are able to work towards the same goals in key moments of mutual reinforcement. Rather than mapping a causal analysis of the impact of think tanks on government policy, this chapter uses think tanks to present a discursive analysis of the contradictory character of techno-populist politics and policy in India.

Exploring the nature of technocratic policymaking in an age of heightened populism reveals underlying tensions between populist demands of 'the people', and elite policymaking experts (Bickerton and Accetti 2017; Buštíková and Guasti 2019). Scholars and political commentators have often offered populism and technocracy as antidotes or correctives to one another. Some propose populist mobilisation as a counter to an increasingly administrative mode of governance, while others (Rosanvallon 2011) advocate for impartial 'independent authorities' to provide complexity to the simplification of democratic legitimacy often brought by populist governments. While technocracy and populism contradict one another in several ways, they share an important characteristic: 'they are both forms of anti-pluralism ... technocrats hold that there's only one correct policy solution; populists claim that there is only one authentic will of the people (and only they represent it); whoever disagrees with them, reveals themselves as traitor to the people' (Müller 2018) .

Think tanks, while a professional home for the technocrats Müller (2018) is referring to, are not necessarily anti-pluralist

---

[2] As mentioned in Chapter 1, I understand technocracy as encompassing a discourse of neutral governance, set of institutions, bureaucratic practices, and a culture of corporate professionalism.

institutions. Yet a growing alignment between a majoritarian right-wing government, an increasingly deracinated technocratic class, and supposedly 'independent' policy institutions can narrow the plurality of expertise they offer and form an 'expert monopoly' (Moore et al. 2020, 17). A majoritarian political bloc may successfully achieve electoral legitimacy, yet representative democratic systems claim to have bodies independent of electoral representatives to act as correctives to political power and democratically legitimate mis-steps. By this, I am referring to the judicial, legislative, and executive separation of powers: particularly the process outlined by Ambedkar (2014, 37) in the post-Independence debates of making India a constitutional democracy.[3] These institutions are necessary to counter a majoritarian democratic state. In their idealised form, they allow for minority protection, constitutional rules to be upheld, and independent thought to build and contribute to a politically diverse public.

This process, however, is increasingly fraught by a growing collusion between political leadership, an alternative authority of valued 'expertise', and corporate interests. Such a nexus exemplifies a key component of populism in power: a transmutation of the democratic principles of popular sovereignty, such that only one part of the people are seen as legitimate (Urbinati 2019). Unlike representative or constitutional democracy, which assumes legislative and procedural systems that are inclusive of all people, populist democracy rejects the notion of generality and embraces representing the 'best part' (Urbinati 2019, 123) that rules openly for its own good, needs, and interests. In doing this, it makes a radical break from the party system, electoral representation, and constitutional democracy, while still using the means of the party in its struggle against established parties. As such, it is 'a regime *of* rather than *by* the majority' (Urbinati 2019, 123).

---

[3] This includes supposedly independent bodies of knowledge production like universities, research organisations, and advisory bodies, and ideally independent knowledge dissemination bodies like the media.

In this chapter, I first give an overview of broad theoretical debates concerning the Indian government's shifting priorities. Using data from in-depth interviews with politicians and policy-makers, I then examine three key discourses in policy expertise. First, several interviews reveal a deep division between policymaking as a rational, technical exercise, and political representation as an irrational, instrumental, and heightened emotional practice. This vision of politics erases the fundamental democratic importance of pluralistic representation or accountability, and furthers the production of insular pragmatism in policymaking. Secondly, technocratic policymakers make appeals to credibility by positioning themselves as 'post-ideology'. They pride themselves in abiding by a rational 'truth', distinct from instrumental self-interest or ideological bias. The latter part of this discourse becomes further complicated with Hindu-nationalist policymakers who intrinsically argue for an ethno-centric civilisational superiority. While these new Hindu-nationalist 'intellectuals' also see their policymaking work as distinct from the 'self', they reason that it moves them towards a higher cause of nationalist unity. Thirdly, I show how the contradictions between technocratic and populist future imaginaries can, in fact, resolve themselves through hybridised discourse and practice. They work together to legitimise an overarching push of Indian global ascendance grounded in a Hindu-nationalist normativity.

I take inspiration from scholarship that has recently theorised the 'diffuse logic' of Hindutva's influence (Anderson and Longkumer 2018; Reddy 2011b). This literature argues that Hindu-nationalist rhetoric can be drawn on by a range of hard-core ideologues, critics, sympathisers, affiliates, and so on to strategically make claims that may be disconnected from Hindutva's ideological core. The BJP can thus remain engaged with a network of both Hindu-nationalist think tanks and economically pragmatic think tanks by opportunistically mobilising Hindu nationalism as a political force in popular politics, while at other times relegating it to fringe cultural practice in technocratic policy discussions. This contradictory approach follows Hansen's (2018) characterisation of anti-politics as a form of politics based in opposition to the prevailing order grounded in secular ideals, to 'denounce *rajkaraan* (politics), to separate the nation and its cultures from the realm of rational statecraft, and to adopt a moral, anti-political critique of political leaders' (Hansen 2018, 229). Rational statecraft in the form of economic pragmatism, then, exists in parallel to a Hindu-nationalist movement that oscillates between being projected as political and at other times anti-political.

THE RISE OF THINK TANK GOVERNANCE

A post-Independence India strived to build a self-reliant economy, where economic development was largely driven by the state. The early Congress government's general suspicion of both foreign and private interests pervaded the internal advisory process for decades after Independence. However, while lobbying as such is stigmatised, the lines between lobbying, advisory capacity, and advocacy are blurry. As such, chambers of commerce and domestic business groups influenced major decisions within economic planning, prioritising protectionism and economic nationalism (Chhibber and Verma 2018; Kaviraj 2010b). Several advisory groups were set up at this time to oversee state planning and allocate budgets to further industrial development.

In the 1980s, scholar Sudipta Kaviraj (1988) argued that a coalitional strategy between the bureaucratic elite, landed agrarian elite, and industrial capitalists (assisted by the licence regime in building monopolies) gave these groups dominance over state-directed processes of economic growth, and the 'allocational necessities indicated by the bourgeois democratic political system' (Kaviraj 1988, 1230). Following economic liberalisation in 1991, the opening up of a range of sectors to foreign and private control has led the corporate class to surpass that of the landed, agrarian elite (Chatterjee 2008). The capitalist class, then, has come to acquire a moral–political dominance over the Indian middle classes that they are able to exercise through elections, media, and the bureaucratic-managerial elite.[4] The managerial elite, consisting of the urban middle classes, has in turn largely disavowed the state as a corrupt, politically opportunistic entity. Its members have effectively moved towards a consensus on the priority of socio-economic growth through the professional and corporate private sector. The engineer, inventor, and entrepreneur Sam Pitroda said in 1993, 'politics, as popularly understood, will take the back seat. Technology will be at the wheel. Technocrats will take precedence over politicians' (Pitroda 1993). While technological modernity is not equivalent to technocratic managerialism, the latter's focus on efficiency, data fetishism, and corporate cultural professionalism often includes technology as a key component.

A moment demonstrating this shift from central state planning to consultant-driven, think tank–oriented governance is the disbanding of the Planning Commission in 2014. Soon after India's Independence, Nehru, India's first prime minister, set up a Planning Commission (PC) consisting of industrialists, technocrats, and economists to allocate funds to ministries and state governments and, as such, oversee state planning and industrial development. For the majority of the last seven decades, this elite body of intellectuals and technocrats has played a formative role in Indian policymaking (Kaviraj 2010a). Its members remained fairly consistent despite electoral shifts in political parties, providing a 'technocratic counterweight' to political changes (Irani 2019, 45). As Partha Chatterjee (1993, 202) notes, this group was meant to rise above 'the squabbles' of petty politics to innovate and develop policy rationally for the 'needy masses' (Irani 2019, 8). When Modi became prime minister in 2014, his administration disbanded the PC and replaced it with the NITI Aayog, a self-described

---

[4] Chatterjee's distinction between political society and civil society addresses the differential routes the modern-corporate class (civil society) and working-informal class (political society) must take in order to make demands from the state in postcolonial India. While the modern-corporate class can address its needs through civic organisations, influence, and pressure, the working-informal class must do so through negotiations and electoral democratic means.

think tank–like organisation stripped of its budget allocation powers and essentially made up of development and management consultants to coordinate state–industry relationships. Effectively, this shift showed the government transitioning its support from an already watered-down version of centralised planning by the intellectual elite, to a 'diffuse entrepreneurship', handing power to those entrepreneurs and innovators who saw development as a market 'opportunity' (Elyachar 2012; Irani 2019, 10).

Parallel to this change in the composition of government-appointed technocrats and experts, the rise of populist discontents played a significant role in the BJP's rise. Fatigue and distrust of the previous political regime, the Congress government, paved the path for deep anti-incumbent sentiment. At the same time, Modi and the BJP built an image in opposition to the Congress' corrupt and elitist political bloc: transparent and accountable, putting the country's well-being above himself, while at the same time being the only person capable of leading it to its full potential. In a million to one chance, he is both the million and the one. He became known as the bringer of development (the *vikaas purush*/'development man'), promising economic progress, an influx of jobs, and financial security. His history of presiding over and fuelling the Gujarat pogrom in 2002, which killed almost a thousand Muslims, was erased, accepted, or rationalised away (Dhattiwala and Biggs 2012). In capitalising on a discourse of corruption, the BJP effectively presented itself as the only alternative: able to fix the state *through* the state.

While the BJP's rule has been characterised by many as populist (Chacko 2018), there are multiple contemporary frameworks for what constitutes populism. Often, the term is used across ideologies, discourses, and political and economic strategies. Populist movements tend to set up an opposition between people and elites, but this can be attributed across the ideological spectrum, to both far-left and far-right actors (Muller 2016). These actors can incorporate elements of technocratic discourse, build loose networks, or tight party discipline. Indeed, scholars have argued (Kelly 2017) that the history of modern populism and the history of modern popular sovereignty are cotermin-ous, simply because modern democratic politics is premised upon claims of the history of popular sovereignty. Yet populism in power, Urbinati (2019) argues, is not necessarily the mobilising of people against the establishment, or an ideology of the people seeking their own emancipation. Rather, populist leaders use anti-establishment imagery to ask people to identify with them and to believe that their support for the leader will help them avenge those who have wronged them. The leader builds himself as a representative of the true people through his direct and permanent communication with them, assisted by electronic media.

Ostensibly, then, Modi's win became a move towards demos and away from technos.[5] Yet at the same time, Modi represented not only [being] one of the people but also a 'grassroots' technocrat: owing to his role in transforming his home state Gujarat into a haven for business investment during his tenure as chief minister. As such, he crosses both worlds of demos and technos, while allowing the creation of a new, alternative intellectual base to flourish and replace the old elite.

THINK TANKS AS CUSTODIANS OF NEW DISCOURSE

Qualifying the Impact of Think Tanks

Scholars have traced how think tanks can build and mobilise ideas to resonate with different groups (Medvetz 2012a) through a balance of building democratic legitimacy, claiming expert authority, and con-structing discursive frameworks about what knowledge matters (Newman and Clarke 2018). The influence of right-wing think tanks like the Heritage Foundation, the Cato Institute, and the American

---

[5] Here, I use the Latin 'demos' to refer to a collective People: ranging from a village, an assembly, and a body of citizens, as in early forms of Athenian democracy (Blackwell 2003). 'Technos' refers to the Latin prefix of 'technocracy', a word coined in 1919 by W. H. Smyth as a name for a new system of government by technical experts who could best advise us how to live, and realise our 'individual aspirations and national purpose' (Atherton 1922, 29).

Enterprise Institute has been studied in American politics since the 1980s, yet the cloaked and centralised nature of policymaking culture in India, combined with the relatively recent entry of think tanks as a medium of political influence, makes it challenging to qualitatively define their 'impact'. A key to answering this question, both theoretically and methodologically, is understanding 'to what extent' I can demonstrate the discursive relevance of studying think tanks. Scholars studying think tanks in Europe (Desai 1994; Plehwe 2006, 2014) and the United States (Domhoff 2010; Fischer 2002; Medvetz 2012b; Rich 2005; Skocpol and Williamson 2016) have argued that such organisations have the ability to form 'discourse coalitions' that mainly serve corporate, elite, or government interests far from notions of public interest. Elitist perspectives on think tanks state that they constitute ruling class/top-down dominant knowledge creation (Domhoff 2010), whereas pluralist perspectives (Polsby 1985) claim that they are just one in a wide variety of interest-group organisations.

While these analyses have their merit in tracing communities of knowledge production, an institutionalist perspective (Medvetz 2012b) understands think tanks as creating and reifying 'epistemic communities' (Haas 1992). Rather than recycling a tautological argument narrowly delineating what a think tank is or does, I follow this perspective to study think tanks as creating epistemic communities. As such, this chapter understands them as a heterogeneous array of organisations with a range of effects, including building influential networks, shaping a political agenda, contributing to policy formation, and assisting in policy implementation (Abelson and Carberry 1997). They bring together political elites, media, corporate leaders, and academics, and through their blurred duality of autonomy and heteronomy are able to transcend the barriers of practical knowledge legitimation given to these other fields.

As primarily elite organisations in a vast and diversely impoverished country, a study of Indian think tanks begs several questions about the nature of knowledge dissemination. Primarily, it leads us to ask whether knowledge produced in relatively narrow elite circles seeps through to a popular consciousness; and, indeed, if not, what purpose it serves in understanding ideological transformation. I do not claim a causal relationship between elite think tanks and popular consciousness, nor do I try to assert the primacy of top-down channels of political mobilisation above others. Many scholars have shown that the BJP–RSS network, for example, functions both from bottom-up forms of mobilisation and relies on grassroots intellectuals (Hansen 2018; Jaffrelot 2015), as well as more recent technological forms of top-down party organisation (particularly through social media and the NaMo app, an app that allows the BJP's top leadership to directly communicate with its workers and supporters) (Singh 2019). While the RSS and the BJP instil a more hierarchical and disciplinary party structure than the Congress Party, the RSS has a strong grassroots base that also works independent of the BJP's political elite. I offer an alternative to tracing the directional causality of think tanks by studying them as a site through which to understand the contradictions between populist demands and technocratic policymaking. Drawing from Bourdieusian theories of causality, I maintain that various variables and elements that are related to one another are not necessarily related through linear or transitive causality (Hilgers and Mangez 2014). That is, a change in one does not necessarily lead to a change in another, yet they carry with them a web of 'philosophical doxa' that bleeds into constituting common sense of an intellectual generation and moment.

This analytical framework of understanding impact highlights the *relational* part of influence: the supply chain of ideas, conversations, and people that gain legitimacy moving through these spaces that filter through (both upwards and downwards) to political elites, media influence, social media groups, and other kinds of religious and civic associations. I am gesturing to *discursive* causality (Banta 2013) rather than positivist or linear causality. While there is plausibly influence to the extent that these organisations operate in networks of the elite, they have not necessarily been active long enough to observe a pattern of linear causality that would be irrefutable.

In arguing for discursive influence, my argument fundamentally counters think tanks' claims of neutral pragmatism in policy solutions, as discourse itself imposes 'categories and paradigms onto the world of experience' (Foucault 2012; Tribe 1972, 76). As such, I note that think tanks contain and assert, through their funding structures, their choices of research topics and the framing of their recommendations deep political and ideological influence. Indeed, throughout the next few chapters, I trace the categories of expertise and intellectual output that are gaining increased relevance to reveal shifts in notions of democratic representation.

The BJP's anti-intellectual majoritarianism, for example, discredits existing (i.e. 'Old Elite') elite intellectuals as irrelevant and detached, while building alternative forms of credible knowledge and expertise (Fischer et al. 2015; Newman and Clarke 2018). The following quote from an interview with the head of a leading think tank explicates the BJP–RSS's two-armed sociocultural agenda: to build both populist support and technocratic expertise.

> What is the BJP's larger or the RSS' socio-cultural agenda? It is to build a new elite into the system. So, the world of universities, academic institutions, think tanks – these are all elite institutions where they want to place their version of elites. So ... even though the RSS has a much, much, much stronger front line and grass-roots connect and there could be a pipeline through which the ideas could actually go from the bottom to the top, in effect, the world of ideas essentially operates in the landscape of elites. And these elites are either the Old Elite which is the Congress World, or the New Elite which is the RSS World. And the New Elites too are trying to build institution spaces for them to continue to influence in precisely the same modes and transactions that the Old Elite had.
>
> (Interview with leading member[6] of the Centre for
> Policy Research, May 2019)

---

[6] Anonymous by request.

The 'Old Elite' is seen to consist of pedigreed, English-speaking, and Western-educated groups of left-liberal academics and public intellectuals with sociocultural capital. As this interviewee notes, the BJP is trying to shift notions of expertise by ousting this 'Old Elite'. Yet, rather than calling on their grassroots network to develop a bottom-up approach to policymaking, they are mainly replacing one elite with another. As Verniers and Jaffrelot (2020) show through an analysis of Lok Sabha assemblies over the years, the demographic composition of elites has diversified as caste-based affirmative action has grown, yet the 'overall elitism of the political class has remained constant' (2020, 10). The New Elite they offer consists of broadly two types of experts: Hindu-nationalist intellectuals who harken to Hindu civilisational superiority, former military chiefs/retired bureaucrats who stand by a highly patriotic, if Hindu nationalist, idea of India; and technical professionals, such as engineers, business managers, and consultants. The former are in favour of the BJP's Hindu-nationalist agenda, while the latter pride themselves on being largely apolitical, but tend to fall in line with the ruling administration's sense of pragmatic rationalism and normative Hindu nationalism. While the BJP claims to replace the Old Elite in the name of ostensibly democratising centres of power, they are primarily reproducing the elite insularity of policymaking processes.

While this chapter critiques such emerging forms of expertise, I do not mean to suggest that the *attempt* towards democratising anointed authority in the realm of policymaking is without merit, or that there are no other challenges to the (new or old) elite bastion of experts in India. Rather, I am arguing that the shift in who are considered the experts is heightening rather than diffusing the elite inwardness of policymaking processes. Indeed, the current political climate in India has led to an intensification of the long-existing[7]

---

[7] Indeed, this chasm is not new; I instead argue that it is being deepened and legitimated in new ways. In a speech delivered to the All-India Trade Unions Workers Camp in 1943, Ambedkar (2014:109) said, 'All political societies get divided into two classes – the Rulers and the Ruled. This is an evil. If the evil stopped here it

chasm between political representation and policymaking, such that authoritative voices of experts continue to operate within structures of power at the root of 'democratic deficits' (Fischer et al. 2015). As Chapter 4 explores, the last decade has seen an increased outsourcing of the democratic process: an outsourcing of bureaucratic governance to think tanks and global management consulting firms (Shrikanth 2019), such as McKinsey, Boston Consulting Group, and Ernst & Young, to name a few, as well as an outsourcing of election campaigns to political consulting firms that use big data to effectively manipulate voters (Singh 2019). An interview with Sachin Rao, the head of training party workers within the Congress Party, reveals the growing alienation of policymaking from popular consciousness:

> In India, our core problem is the inadequacy of politicisation and equity of participation. This scares me. It's inhuman. It's a travesty of humanity to leave people without agency and outside of conversations. So the problem to me is not how we design a better school, but how we make the voice of the person who's sitting in that village an effective instrument of change. Now, rather than working on this, we've made our focus on think tanks – our class's cop out of using our prestige and our degrees to produce ideas that we inject at very high levels of the execution space.

I use Indian think tanks as a focal point to understand the diverse sites where authoritative knowledge of various kinds is produced and, to use Rao's terminology, how such ideas are sold. What I characterise as 'think tanks' are, in effect, organisations that house old and new policy experts. These people and organisations fit into a supply chain of ideas at a crucial level. They build affective ties between various parts of the old and new elite, marking the stamp of 'expertise' onto

would not matter much. But the unfortunate part of it is that the division becomes stereotyped and stratified so much so that the Rulers are always drawn from the Ruling Class and the class of the Ruled never becomes the Ruling class. People do not govern themselves, they establish a government and leave it to govern them, forgetting that it is not their government.'

certain ideas that are then mobilised to propagate certain concerns more than others.

> As opposed to investing, building a polity and fraternity – we bypass the whole thing, even as we pay lip service to the constitution. Now because polity itself has shrunk towards electioneering, brand management, it's a game show kind of space with very little depth and people connect. So in that gap, you have all kinds of people who are selling all kinds of products. From think tanks who are selling ideas, to brand managers who are selling perceptions, to execution managers who are actually outsourcing the entire process of elections. So in a sense, polity has abdicated its responsibility of mass politicisation, of representing people. So in those gaps, and the weakening process of fraternity, [and] exchanging ideas and conversation – that's where all of these think tanks have come about.
>
> *(Interview with Sachin Rao, training-in-charge of Congress Party)*

As such, they lend a 'technical mystique' to ideas, masking underlying power dynamics by enveloping experts with an aura of objective rationality (Fischer et al. 2015). Historically, the glorification of technocratic and technological expertise has transcended the traditional left-right divide (Bustikova and Guasti 2019). This has allowed proponents of this expertise to claim a non-partisan, anti-political pragmatism. My interviews show that experts' ideological underpinnings become increasingly muted as they build networks and reinforce one another's basic assumptions. Ideology, in this case, seeks to 'masquerade as analysis, deriving a power it could never justly claim from the garb of neutrality it has at times contrived to wear' (Tribe 1972, 66). One interviewee who is a key member of the Vivekananda International Foundation points at the 'intermingling' at the core of elite knowledge networks:

> The other interesting thing is that there's a large intermingling of the think tanks that sit – the same people are circulating, we know

each other, we've worked together in the government, and in the end everybody wants good for India. As a group, even though we haven't organised ourselves as a group, we attend each other's meetings and seminars and in that way harmonised coordinated positions occur. So very often you will find that if you discuss the same issues in a few iterations over the years, most think tanks will start thinking in a similar way ...

(Interview with representative from Vivekananda International Foundation,[8] a BJP-affiliated think tank, May 2019)

As this quote demonstrates, the events held by think tanks tend to bring together a range of old and new influential political, bureaucratic, and corporate elites. In creating tangible spaces that allow for this mutual exchange of knowledge, they effectively mediate processes of social networking. Attendees at these events are able to converse and enter a dialogue that leads their ideas to make more sense. Particular paradigms of common sense become written into their meeting grounds with shared assumptions about what is 'good for India' (that is, a Bourdieusian technocratic doxa). Even if some measure of dissensus persists, the ambit of topics that are discussed and the range of opinions that people express becomes limited (what Palshikar (2020) describes as an ideological hegemony of governance). An interviewee formerly within the EAC-PM argued that 'unlike in the West, deep ties between people in India are not transactional'. Their ties become stronger when they attend events together and interact at a personal level. These strong ties then evolve into stronger social kinships (where most members share a class and caste position) that make it more likely that ideas that are shared in these spaces will 'feel' right. This is particularly where the distinction between formal processes of politics and policymaking and informal, intangible influence become essential (Medvetz 2006; Schildt et al. 2019). Here, then, a cohort of authoritative experts are working on multiple levels. They

---

[8] Anonymous by request.

are (a) discrediting existing research organisations and creating their own institutions; (b) building affective ties with the existing institutions and experts who are willing to acquiesce to their normative assumptions.

BJP's Expanding Policy Network

The Bharatiya Janata Party's (BJP) landslide wins in 2014 and in 2019 were a result of several immediate and accumulated events that resulted in building a strong coalition of support. The BJP promised widespread social mobility, financial independence, and job growth. It mobilised a rhetoric of self-reliance and Hindu strength to promote aggressive national security in the face of external and internal threats (Jaffrelot 2015). However, the BJP is not a monolith. Its political strategies to build support are varied and at times inconsistent, but crucially interspersing Hindutva and economic development. Part of its political strategy has been putting together its own ecosystem of policymakers in think tanks. The following excerpt from an interview with a BJP leader of knowledge production exemplifies how they attempt to build ideological support through policy networks.

> One [of our tasks] is to analyse, interpret and disseminate it to a larger intelligentsia ... For us the work is amongst people, we do a lot of political ideological work as well as policy work. We have round tables and controlled programs, but we also have bigger programs, where you want to make an ideological political point but through the route of policy.
>
> (Interview with Anirban Ganguly, head of Dr Syama Prasad Mookerjee Research Foundation, a BJP-affiliated think tank, March 2019)

In 2014, the BJP won by a majority, and members of their think tanks assumed key positions within the central government. This conjuncture of events suggests a deliberate strategy towards ideological hegemony in Delhi's policy world, yet it is also something that routinely happens in democracies. Thus, it raises broader theoretical questions about institutions affecting political change: is it mass

consumption of ideas that leads to political shifts, or rather the deliberate and strategic channelling of them towards a confluence of
powerful ears? In the Indian case, think tanks attempt to use both:
they channel their ideas through convening events and roundtables
with powerful politicians, bureaucrats, and industrialists; present
briefs to ministers in private, informal gatherings; and hold public
events with the media to disseminate their ideas to a larger group of
people. However, the demographic that is able to access the research
output of these think tanks is limited to an English-speaking middle-
class elite. As such, they most fruitfully disseminate their ideas
through strategically building networks with influential members of
the political elite, who are then able to target these messages to a
broader audience. An interview with Ram Madhav, the former
National General Secretary of the BJP, reveals that the BJP uses their
think tanks to build channels of influence within elite networks of
the policymaking ecosystem:

> In India that conscience is growing – thinking, intellectual
> conferencing. It helps us, reaching out to them, then slowly
> bringing them closer to BJP thinking, what we think. That's also
> useful for us. We get so many new people who connect with our
> party and our government through our think tanks.
>
> *(Interview with Ram Madhav, former National General Secretary of BJP*
> *and President of India Foundation, February 2019)*

While I elaborate on Hindu-nationalist intellectuals further in this
chapter, Chapter 5 addresses more specifically the BJP's modes of
influence through its think tanks.

A TYPOLOGY OF INDIAN THINK TANKS

While think tanks have become an established part of policymaking
in the United States and Europe, Indian think tanks are still in their
early stages. Research organisations have existed for several decades
as far back as the 1960s, yet they were rarely called 'think tanks'. The
term is borrowed from an American historical context and has only

become a more popular descriptor in India over the last decade. In fact, many of my interviewees in older, more established research organisations objected to being called 'think tanks', as they see think tanks as pursuing a superficial networking and event-planning role rather than one of core academic research. While this is a somewhat peripheral semantic issue, it reflects a wider professionalisation of the policy research space. In this vein, think tanks have been mushrooming over the last decade, making India the country with the second largest number of think tanks in the world (second only to the United States). As shown in Figure 3.1, while there were approximately 100 think tanks in 2008, they rose to more than 500 in 2018. The number of think tanks briefly dropped in 2014 (soon after Modi was elected, the BJP government cracked down on civil society organisations with foreign funding), but have risen dramatically between 2016 and 2020.

There are broadly three types of think tanks that are considered to have a seat at the decision-making table: (1) government-funded/ affiliated to ministries; (2) privately funded; (3) think tanks attached to political parties (these may not identify themselves as think tanks but serve the purpose of external research-based advisors). Government-affiliated think tanks tend to move between heteronomy and autonomy, varying the nature of research they produce. These think tanks are often funded partly or wholly by the government and develop research agendas in consultation with the ministry to which they are attached. The think tank's research specialisations play a role in its output: there is, across the political spectrum, a hawkish tendency to most foreign policy think tanks that argue from the point of view of uncompromising patriotism, whereas economic policy think tanks tend to rely on the legitimacy of technocratic expertise, and purposely distance themselves from political or ideological partisanship.

The second type, the corporate, privately funded think tanks, mostly emphasise a rationalist division between the individual experts and their research output, relying on notions of fiscal pragmatism and technocratic logic. A key example here is the Observer

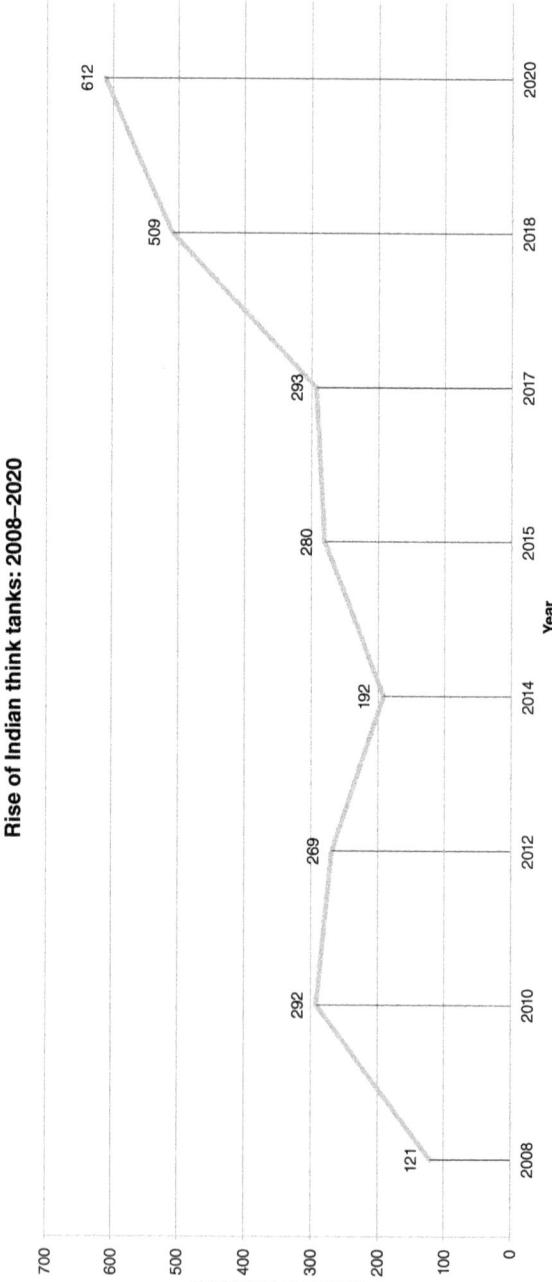

FIGURE 3.1 Data on rise of Indian think tanks
(*Source:* McGann 2020)

Research Foundation (ORF), India's largest think tank funded by Reliance Industries and Mukesh Ambani, the richest man in Asia. ORF was established after India's economic liberalisation in the 1990s and serves, primarily, to hold convening events for the country's most prosperous and influential industrialists, politicians, and bureaucrats. As such, its intellectual output is marginal in comparison to its relational, network-building machinery.

The third kind of think tank refers to entities such as the Vivekananda International Foundation (VIF) and India Foundation (IF), both BJP-affiliated think tanks, established mainly between 2008 and 2011. These think tanks outwardly claim to have no driving ideology, but ride on the professed mentality that 'India First' is their leading motivation. Intellectuals at these think tanks also consider themselves to be transcending the individual self while representing the interests of the entire nation – or rather, what the BJP perceives to be in the nation's interest. As Ram Madhav has claimed, policy and nationalism collide through overarching conceptions of national interest:

> Essentially the party's ideology is very important. For example, our party stands on the strong ideology of Nation First, we call it nationalism, call it patriotism, whatever name you give it.
> So everything we develop into a policy is looked at from this prism, what is beneficial to the country at large. We look at national interest first, not even at the party interest, but we are looking at the national interest. Then we make certain important interventions.
>
> *(Interview with Ram Madhav, former National General Secretary of the BJP, February 2019)*

An interview with a founding member of India Foundation shows how the hallowed ground of intellectual credibility permeates notions of authoritative knowledge, regardless of political partisanship. He asserts that Indians continue to primarily respect upper-caste, Brahmanical knowledge production:

> The problem of this country is that [it] has got a Brahmanical
> society purely embedded in it ... the man with the idea is always
> the person with whom everybody wants to be associated ...
> everyone wants to sit with the wise man. *Toh India ke andar think
> tank toh inke DNA mein hai. Iss desh ke DNA mein think tank
> hai.* [India has think tanks in its DNA.] He's taking you beyond
> your current existence. So ideas, the power of ideas. And the power
> of ideas in this country is very fertile so it is natural ... and it is also
> good because it goes with the natural grains of this country.
> *(Interview with representative from India Foundation, May 2019[9])*

Think tanks disseminate their ideas through the media, and through formal and informal meetings with influential politicians and policy-makers. These ideas, then, build a certain level of consensus amongst networks of elites who spread them through top-down movements of echo chambers. In an ostensibly independent think tank, this can create a perception of a space that exists outside of ideology and political party affiliation. Regardless of accusations (and occasional ownership) of bias, think tanks treat their research output as sacral in terms of their intellectual rigour. These claims to credibility are structured differently: whether as moral claims, technical claims, and/or evidence-based claims, which tend to resonate differently based on how different kinds of so-called expertise are valued (Irani 2019). My interviewees presented key distinctions between their evi-dentiary claims – techno-scientific; activist-political; scholarly-intellectual; moral-ideological; and party-partisan.

Economic policy think tanks tend to stake claim to 'truth' and rational choice, where 'crucial choices are essentially technical in character' (Tribe 1972), towards a set of largely agreed settled ends. In this case, that tends to be economic growth, the ambition of development, and technologically-oriented global ascendance. Think tanks and political parties, then, can use contradictory claims

---

[9] Anonymous by request.

together to target different groups of people through different means. Think tanks provide authority and credibility to policy ideas, while the political party can frame them in a way to appeal to popular demands, even when these demands contradict the offered policy solution (Siddiqui 2012).

While escalating the privatisation of public goods, the BJP's rhetoric paradoxically sells these shifts as an increase in state welfare and paternalism (see Chapter 2). As such, a single policy project can use multiple forms of these claims to target different groups: for example, several welfare programmes channel popular demands (such as universal healthcare) to provide democratic legitimacy to policies that enable a continued dominance of political and economic elites (i.e. promising universal healthcare through incentivising private insurance companies). Thus, while the BJP may be 'populist' to the extent that it attempts to build a rigid and unified ethno-nationalist sense of 'us' to take down the 'them' who have led the country astray, their economic policy paradigms are not that different from the Congress Party before them. They follow a largely similar path towards the provision of services and welfare through incentivising the private sector. As such, while the BJP may be changing dominant notions of expertise and instating their own intellectuals, the new authoritative experts continue to reinforce neoliberal economic visions.

'Post'-ideological Policy

Since the economic policies of the major national parties have followed similar paths since 1991, policymakers often pronounce Indian politics as lacking coherent ideological frameworks (Chhibber and Verma 2018; Kohli 2012). Despite the BJP having pockets of protectionist and anti-globalization philosophies (for example, the Swadeshi Jagran Manch, an internal faction, promotes 'national self-reliance' and fights 'economic imperialism'), both major national parties have supported the push towards pro-market policy in the last few decades (see Chapter 2) (Chhibber and Verma 2018). In an interview, a senior Congress MP suggested that we are now in a

'post-ideology' era of political mobilisation. He noted that 'mobilisation happens in poetry, whereas governance happens in prose' and
that these are two distinct modes of building a resonant narrative.
The latter, in particular, is where an upper level of bureaucrats,
policymakers, and policy influencers participate. The following
excerpt illuminates the lines of ideology he draws between politics
and policy.

JR: You know, there is no doubt in my mind that there has
been a shift in the dominant consensus. Now why this
shift has taken place, it's more problematic. We know it
has taken place, but why it has taken place and what are
the channels by which it has taken place, that ... it's not
a Thatcherite kind of [moment] where somebody came
and said, I'm going to demolish [public institutions] ...
Mr. Modi's language today is the language of the state,
you know, state intervention. So I think we're in a post-
ideology world.

Researcher: What do you mean by that?

JR: Where ideologies do not drive political parties. That's
over. That era is over. Ideology drove Thatcher. Ideology
drove Reagan. After that, finished. Ideology drove the
Labour Party. Ideology drove Nehru. Indira Gandhi was
not an ideologue – from 67–77, she was left wing. From
1980–1984, she was right wing. She was no ideologue.

Researcher: So what do you think drives it, if not ideology?

JR: Pragmatism, you know, the sense that ... I mean, people
are less ideological today. Ideology doesn't drive
discourse, the time that used to happen in the 40s and
50s – ideological fears, ideological divides. I wonder
whether it could be the collapse of the Soviet Union
that has something to do with it. I think ideologically
we're all very elastic ... we keep using the phrase 'party
ideology', but I don't see ourselves [that way]. I see us

having a dominant social ideology, but I don't see us having a dominant economic ideology. Our economic ideology is a little more pragmatic, you know. So I think the ideological divides in Indian political discourse now are not economic. The ideological divide is social.

(Interview with Jairam Ramesh, former minister and MP of the Congress Party, January 2019)

This dynamic relationship between politics and policy-making makes starkly clear the distance between popular representation and policymaking. Indeed, it emphasises the legitimacy given to discourses of rationally calculated and purely technical policy decisions as 'pragmatic', while casting aside the role of politics and pluralistic representation beyond reductive notions of 'ideology'. Yet, the clear distinction Ramesh draws between social and economic policy, and the technocratic neutrality of 'post'-ideological economic policy, is itself an ideological accomplishment. The technocratic legitimacy given to notions of pragmatic policymaking is rooted in the Indian state's growing dependence on the private sector, and the relatively greater value attributed to private expertise (Corbridge and Harriss 2013). This form of 'post-ideology' borrows from Swyngedouw's conception of 'post-politics' as 'marked by the predominance of a managerial logic in all aspects of life, the reduction of the political to administration where decision-making is increasingly considered to be a question of expert knowledge and not of political position' (Swyngedouw 2010, 225). Over the last few decades, this has given rise to a 'home-grown' technocracy grounded in paradigms of private business and a sturdy state-business alliance (Kohli 2012). As a leading member of a think tank noted:

> In India, the public-private partnership story was part of this global narrative where private provisioning was seen as a way of streamlining and cleaning up. It was legitimised basically by saying that the state capacity to deliver is limited and therefore

privatisation or adopting private sector principles is the best way in which you can get the state to function better. Therefore, even for core public services, the private-public partnership is an appropriate mode of provisioning.

(Interview with leading member of Centre for Policy Research,[10] May 2019)

As such, private, technical expertise began to be seen as a 'cleaner' alternative to state-sanctioned experts. According to the director of a leading economic policy think tank, the government has moved from providing goods and services to facilitating the private sector, and so has a greater need for more technical expertise:

I think the role of the government in India is changing. And therefore it needs a lot more advice. It needs policy. Because, we are no longer the public sector dominated economy that we were in the 70s and the 80s. Now, along with that the shift towards the private sector means that the role of the government has changed from being a producer of goods and services. And given that they have to do strategic thinking of managing the economy here and now, they need a lot more technical expertise.

(Interview with Rajat Kathuria, Senior Visiting Professor and former Director of Indian Council for Research on International Economic Relations (ICRIER), May 2019)

Kathuria's insistence that the economy needs more private and technical expertise is reflected in the changing actors who shape forms of pragmatic policymaking. Increased globalisation and a growing perception of the complexity of technology, governance, and global security challenges have led to the state outsourcing its policymaking to external, private organisations. Studying how policy organisations can draw frontiers of inclusion and exclusion, Howarth (2010) argues that think tanks can build as well as naturalise dominant hegemonic forms of social relations and knowledge. In India, think-tanks, global consulting firms and chambers of commerce are being hired to

---

[10] Anonymous by request.

provide stagnating bureaucrats and new political leadership with innovative policy ideas. The hyper-technocratic participation of think tanks and management consulting firms, when articulated at the level of governance, threatens to replace, or rather, obfuscate politics itself: 'conflict' and 'struggle' over imbalances of power and structural inequalities and those between competing ideologies – the essence of politics – are eschewed, in the belief that everything can be reduced to 'what works best' (Andrews 2003). An interview with the conservative intellectual I quote at the beginning of this chapter, Swapan Dasgupta, shows that this shift towards policy as an unquestioned technocratic exercise is being actively perpetuated by the BJP:

SD: You know it's becoming more and more that people seem to think the technocratic expertise is really what is needed, and the manner in which these civil services examinations are being structured. There's a great emphasis on that.

Researcher: Do you think that's a shift? Or do you think it's always kind of been that way?

SD: There's been a shift. There's been a shift, and there's a sort of suspicion of generalists ... you're getting people out of college and moulding them and developing their expertise, it may not be articulated as such, but that's what's happening.

(Interview with Swapan Dasgupta, Former BJP MP, February 2019)

Dasgupta talks about 'moulding' young graduates, referencing how many influential think tanks attempt to foster young policymakers through frequent summer internship programmes and youth workshops. The India Foundation, for example, runs the Kautilya Fellowship Programme in association with the Ministry of External Affairs. This workshop teaches a wide range of science, engineering, and management graduates about public policy and includes a pilgrimage to the Kumbh Mela, the largest Hindu religious congregation in India.

Legitimating Hindu-Nationalist Expertise

While some think tanks are explicit about their political and ideological leanings, others claim neutrality, yet practise their bias in euphemisms and coded language. Their key is to effect a change in thinking by normalising it. Part of the BJP's rhetoric is to replace an old pedigreed elite with what they consider as more 'grounded' expertise: both in terms of policy as well as culturally – that is, who understands the needs of the people and is an 'authentic' nationalist (Newman and Clarke 2018). Praveen Chakravarty, the former head of Data Analytics in the Congress Party, justifies the BJP's opposition to 'ivory tower' intellectuals:

> I think the disdain is because of this ivory tower kind of discourse of intellectuals that we've seen. I don't think anyone disagrees with the need for expert opinion, but before we get that, I can understand why the BJP wants to do what it's doing, which is that, 'none of these guys get India' according to them. I don't know if you've seen the cabinet note that led to the formation of NITI Aayog, it actually says a western economic principle does not work for us, we need our own.
>
> *(Interview with Praveen Chakravarty, former head of Data Analytics in the Congress Party, February 2019)*

The discrediting of the old elite as isolated from the 'people' marks the way for the entry of a new set of leaders who are seen by the establishment to 'actually understand' the country. Indeed, policy professionalisation is taking over government ministries. When the BJP came to power in 2014, the government disbanded the Planning Commission and replaced it with the NITI Aayog, an advisory council consisting mainly of former employees from management consulting firms and private industry. As Swapan Dasgupta notes,

> NITI Aayog is a combination of a think tank and a McKinsey – it's a problem solver. Here is an issue, we go in there and, like what McKinsey does, we study the issue, and we give you a set of

recommendations. So the NITI Aayog, at least as it was envisaged, is less to do with macro ideas, and more to do with actual project or scheme management.

(Interview with Swapan Dasgupta, former BJP MP, February 2019)

This, then, has become the primary paradigm of thinking about governance: policy is seen as being 'post-ideology', which claims to have no culture, ideology, or bias apart from pragmatically 'what works best'. Yet this discursive emptiness, as such, allows political leaders to align a rhetoric of glorified technocratic expertise with hyper-nationalist sentiments of indigenous (Hindu) strength. For example, Modi's push towards India having a $5 trillion economy by 2025 is tied into a larger narrative about India's superior economic 'strength' and glory on the global stage. This heightened nationalist pride aligns with the identity politics of the BJP's Hindu India.

I am not implying that technocratic post-ideology policy and Hindu nationalism are inherently tied together, nor that the former is entirely a tool for the latter. These two discursive worlds are not inherently entwined; indeed, in some sense they are contradictory. The latter focuses primarily on culture, caste, and religion, attempting to build a rigid national identity, whereas the former claims to have no culture. Hence it can be used in the service of the latter, as bolstering claims to a grand national and technological future, diagnosing concerns and solutions as neutral and 'post-ideological'. As research has shown, technocratic primacy is able to reinforce nationalist claims to future glory, global standing, and efficient delivery systems (Centeno 2010). At the same time, the BJP's ethnocentric nationalism has solidified the majoritarian population's trust in the central leadership, allowing for a deeper integration of technological systems in citizens' lives. This is often (but not necessarily) in the form of surveillance, and can only be achieved if the (majority of) the population places speculative trust in the ruling party's ability to govern them.

Paradoxically, while an acultural discourse of technical expertise claims credibility through its distance from political ideology,

Hindu civilisational expertise is also gaining legitimacy in policy discussions. Hindu-nationalist think tanks follow the BJP's populist rhetoric by professing to decolonize knowledge, yet, instead, they merely transfer knowledge-making power from a set of English-speaking post-colonial elite to a set of largely upper-caste Hindu elite. An interview with the former head of the Vivekananda International Foundation showcases that Indian culture and policy needs to harken back to its strong civilisational roots in order to succeed:

> India was so advanced at a point of time, and then for 1000 years there's nothing. Why did that happen? Because we forgot about Indianness. You look at Russia, they still speak in Russian, you and I speak in English. You look at Germans, they speak in German, you look at Americans, they have hardly any history but look at how they talk about American exceptionalism. Look at the Chinese. So it is very important to develop an Indian narrative or being Indian. That doesn't mean that you shut yourself off, even if you look at Rabindranath Tagore, Gandhi, Gokhale, Tilak, Savarkar, Syama Prasad Mukherjee, Radhakrishnan, all these people were at heart deeply Indian and very concerned that Western values and culture were becoming too dominant and driving away our own creativity ... And you'll realise that India has a very rich thinking starting from Vedas, scriptures, Ramayan, epics, etc., contribution to science, technology, advanced thinking, literature, philosophy, music, and even skills. If you look at the Veda there are 74 skills listed there.

Our interviewee is expressing a specific discourse of anti-imperialist and nationalist pride. Indian nationalism has several forms, yet this quote animates and anchors a Hindu civilisational, ethnocentric trope.

> So this thing was all forgotten. Then you had a strong influence of the leftist historians who said all this was hocus-pocus. What is this *maathe pe tilak laga diya* [putting a 'tilak' (mark) on your forehead

to indicate religious membership], you do this *puja* [prayer], all this is material forces, and Indians never really had that greatness, there is no historical record of any of this, it's all mythology. This kind of thinking which was encouraged by the British generated a lot of inferiority complexes in Indians and still exists.

(Interview with former head of Vivekananda International Foundation,[11]
a BJP-affiliated think tank, May 2019)

There is a potential contradiction here in future visions of national imaginaries: one as wholly culturally Hindu, eschewing modern forms of Western progress, including technological advancement, and the other as wholly technical.[12] However, the BJP glosses over these contradictions through forms of political discourse that are strategically targeted to resonate with different normative moral and political concerns. Both the production of pragmatism in technocratic economic policy and also the emotive power of nationalism allow for parallel forms of emotional and cognitive resonance. The ideological goal here is twofold: to unite the population with a dominant nationalist conception of the 'authentic Indian', and to simultaneously bolster forms of development to claim technological glory. The two world views often function independently too: the technocratic turn has been growing since liberalisation, and the nationalist imaginary of India as a Hindu civilisation has brought about a majoritarian state. Indeed, as Anirban Ganguly, the head of a BJP policy organisation, notes, the notion of 'Indian exceptionalism' strengthens the discourse of the BJP's rule:

It's very emotionally resonant, and the people in general get to know – it's part of our cultural policy, it's a reflection of our

---

[11] Anonymous by request.
[12] There is also an argument that ancient India was already technologically advanced in the sciences, maths, and engineering. Part of the BJP and RSS's project is to recover the glory of this civilisational technical prowess. Yet this adopted binary of Western versus Indic science is vague and makes it unclear where certain kinds of technical and technological prowess fall.

aspiration to see India emerge as a great power, and also a reflection of our conviction that India is a civilizational power. So ... all these things fall into that larger rubric where you change the discourse and the narrative largely alters. This concept of Indian exceptionalism – what Modi has done in the last five years in terms of a cultural narrative is to release the thought that as Indians we are exceptional. Just this thought.

(Interview with Anirban Ganguly, head of Dr Syama Prasad Mookerjee Research Foundation, March 2019)

These otherwise inconsistent narratives of technical expertise and populist, Hindu-nationalist sentiments are able to persist by avoiding confronting their contradictions, as well as reinforcing one another when necessary. As different narratives target particular constituencies, the discursive points of unity require suppressing parts of each narrative. In certain situations, an ethnocentric hyper-nationalism is partly coded through a rhetoric of development that requires technical and technocratic expertise. The Indian occupation, enforced curfew, and communication blackout of Muslim-dominated Kashmir from August 2019 has been justified through a claim towards bringing long-awaited economic development to the region. In this case, the argument to spread economic, technocratic development is used to justify a Hindu-nationalist desire for global ascendance and the occupation of contested territories. The concept of development, as many scholars have noted, has always been durable and easily attached to several causes: 'from colonisation to anti-colonial nationalism, from market imperialism to state socialism, and from left-wing populism to right-wing populism' (V. Gidwani, personal communication, 2020). At the same time, as my interviewees demonstrate, not everyone sees economic pragmatism as being married to Hindu nationalism. In fact, one of the key attributes of this form of 'diffuse' neo-Hindutva (Reddy 2018) is that Hindu nationalism and its offshoots are often seen as anti-political and primarily cultural such that they become an orthodox form of nationalism.

CONCLUSION: DEMOS AND TECHNOS

Since its overwhelming victory in 2014, the BJP has combined an ideology of Hindu and Indian superiority and self-reliance with discourses of empowerment through global capital. As this chapter has argued and the next one builds on, when conversations become framed as administration by rational judgement (Bell 1976), this tends to leave out conversations around alternative political visions in liberal democratic frameworks: minority protection, constitutional rights, varied political publics, the democratic process, and the potential pitfalls of a democratic majoritarianism. Often-repeated paradigms of thought valuing the same tools of measurement, outcome, and results cease to be perceived as ideological.

In many ways, the transfer of advisory positions from an older rule of experts to a new rule of different experts simply exacerbates a 'post-ideological' rule from above. The BJP is able to mobilise its political base through ethno-nationalist promises, while simultaneously appealing to a range of more moderate demographics through its emphasis on pragmatic economic policy. In some cases, such as with its occupation of Kashmir in the name of development, and its projection of the Kumbh Mela and Yoga Day as signs of infrastructural progress, it is able to marry both imperatives. In other cases, it allows for a diffuse posturing of an anti-political Hindutva that gains its strength from infusing everyday forms of citizenship towards a generalisable national ethos (Anderson and Longkumer 2018).

Outsourcing Democracy through Professional Consulting

In India, generations of upper caste, elite educated, and mostly Hindu men have filled positions of power, including parliamentary seats, administrative services, business groups, advisory boards, and chambers of commerce. While the composition of India's political and bureaucratic elites has diversified since the 1980s as a result of caste-based affirmative action, the elitism of the political classes as a whole has remained a constant (Verniers and Jaffrelot 2020). In 2014, repeated charges of corruption against the Congress Party and a growing anti-intellectual political discourse led to popular discrediting of the central bureaucracy and a sharp stigmatisation of elite policymakers. Sociocultural elite intellectuals, economists, and academics began to be perceived as insular from the needs of 'the people'. Modi and the BJP, then, won the national election by appealing to sentiments of being one of 'the people' and positioning themselves as lacking the instrumental self-interest associated with other political parties.

Simultaneously, a nationalist discourse of a New, Digital India boasted great technical and technological home-grown expertise, proliferating a form of 'entrepreneurial citizenship' (Irani 2019) in which cosmopolitan Indians are urged to see governance as an opportunity to design, innovate, and produce market value as a form of nation-building. This has catalysed a restructuring of people working within decision-making centres of policy and politics. Elite intellectuals and Western-educated economists holding political and policymaking power are being replaced by technical, white-collar 'professionals': engineers, business managers, and consultants. This group of

94

professionals is seen to be a politically agnostic, rational, and practical source of business-minded knowledge in opposition to intellectually insular elites. Paradoxically, however, this shift is transferring power from one set of 'intellectual' experts to an equally elite, deracinated group of professional consultants situated in global management consulting firms (such as McKinsey, Ernst & Young, and PricewaterhouseCoopers).

As Chapter 3 suggests, a key symbolic moment demonstrating this shift is the disbanding of the Planning Commission in 2014. Soon after India's Independence, the first prime minister set up a Planning Commission (PC) consisting of industrialists, technocrats, and economists to oversee state planning and industrial development. For the majority of the last seven decades, this elite body of intellectuals and technocrats has played a formative role in Indian policymaking. Issues of development were withdrawn from public arenas of discussion and 'surrendered to so-called expert groups, creating a sort of elite confidentiality around vital decisions about politics and society' (Kaviraj 2010a, 29). When Modi became prime minister in 2014, his administration disbanded the PC and replaced it with the NITI Aayog, a consultant-heavy think tank. Effectively, this shift showed the government transitioning its support from a watered-down version of centralised planning to handing power to those entrepreneurs and professionals who saw development as a market opportunity (Elyachar 2012; Irani 2019).

In this context, this chapter builds on the previous one to interrogate the marketising of politics and policymaking in India: in particular, the new social imaginaries and normative vocabularies that fuel and sustain it. Previous scholarship studying public sector reforms (Clarke and Newman 1997; Davies 2003; Desai and Imrie 1998; Klikauer 2013; Kohli 2012; Saint-Martin 2004; Sivaramakrishnan 2012) charts the rise of a 'new' managerialism within government bureaucracies and the growth of technocratic paradigms in institutions of global governance. More recently, scholars have called for renewed attention to apolitical forms of politics in India that are characterised by outsourcing governance and political activities to technical consultants (Anderson and Longkumer 2018; Reddy 2011b; Udupa 2018a). Following some of these scholars, I am careful to not dismiss such manifestations of apolitical behaviour as disingenuous, but rather seek to address their motivations and effects. I build on this by examining the political discourses that *legitimate* the shift of power and expertise to an elite group of technocratic consultants. In particular, I seek to make sense of the material and discursive problems that professional consultants are hired to fix in a broken and stigmatised democratic system.

To make this argument, I revisit the symbolic divide between notions of 'politics' and 'policy' from Chapter 3. A key building block in the production of new forms of political and policy governance is the growing influence of political and policy consulting firms. Analytically, I conceptualise two interconnected but distinct domains: the *'policy market'* and the *'election market'*. I understand these two markets as separate, with different key actors and organisations competing within both. Yet a key reason they maintain this separation is the investment of policymakers in seeing 'politics' and 'policy' as two different realms. This distinction allows policymakers to perceive managerial actors (whether in government institutions or private organisations) as technocratic and rational, in opposition to irrational political play, ideology, and inveterate bureaucracy. While the populist pushback to an old rule of experts claimed to bring about less insular systems of policymaking, this desire to see policy as necessarily rational and pragmatic fuels the shift of power from elite intellectuals and experts over to even more insular and disconnected management consultants. The two markets consist of organisations and actors competing with each other through formal and informal means to sell policy priorities to the government and to voters. While participating in governance in overlapping ways, they represent distinct types of professionals, motivations, and beliefs about the state.

After making the implications of this shift clear, I will show how the distinction between 'messy' politics and 'rational' policy is

slowly breaking down as more technocratic professionals, often rele-
gated to policy consulting, work on political election campaigns.
Political consultants are being hired by political parties to manage
election campaigns and 'clean up' politics. The exponential growth of
political consulting firms in the last ten years creates an alternative
mode of political and civic participation that is valued precisely
because it is perceived as politically neutral. Political consultants
see themselves as working with particular political parties to bring
about a 'stable and good' government structure. While eschewing
ideological partisanship, they pursue what they see as a universal
common good through a different lens: one predicated on electing
political parties that are committed to market stability. This notion
of 'good' liberal governance brings about a new mentality towards
'public good'. Governmental effectiveness, in this framework, is
measured by economic rather than political terms, where 'the market
must tell the truth: it must tell the truth in relation to governmental
practice' (Betta 2016; Foucault et al. 2008). A 'good and stable' government, then, is one that must guarantee proper and free economic
activity to contribute to public good.

Based on my interviews, I examine how several of the professional consultants who spoke to me claim a distinct form of 'creative'
rationalism (Andrews 2003). Their distance from politics-as-usual and
stringent bureaucratic processes makes their decisions appear more
universally pragmatic. In addition, a number of these young professionals see their work as *remaking* meanings of civic participation.
This reflexivity, rather than illusory, has a productive discursive
power. It builds and reinforces an industry that sees political ideology
as limited by self-interest, idealism, and/or coherent, but confining,
systems of thought. In turn, they see themselves as 'post ideological'
and pursuing a much-needed pragmatic rationalism in governance. As
Irani's (2019) notion of 'entrepreneurial' citizenship argues, such pragmatism is not simply a limited technical approach to problem solving,
but attempts to enact a diversity of creative and cultural perspectives
through which to produce market value.

While technical professionals are being increasingly privileged in decision-making, the categories of 'professional' and 'intellectual' I am drawing here are by no means discrete. Rather, I am emphasising the key distinction in how they are perceived by the communities I study, and how these perceptions strengthen discourses of political transformation: the *professional* is seen as rational, meritocratic, and possessing tangible technical skills, and the *intellectual* as (often) Western-educated, elite, insular, and too abstract. This political discourse relies on the creation of binaries: an interview with a high-ranking government bureaucrat told me that academics, intellectuals, and economists are seen as the 'thinkers', while technical professionals are the 'implementers'. What the country needs, he noted, is the implementers. Indeed, several actors cross over and occupy roles in overlapping spheres, particularly if their educational training and professional experience allows them to do so.

Though this chapter implies a normative critique of outsourcing to consulting firms, I do not claim that politicians, bureaucrats, intellectuals, and/or academics are necessarily more responsive to the needs of a diverse political citizenry, or more driven by concerns of a plural 'common good', as some scholars have suggested (Putnam 1977; Sivaramakrishnan 2012). Neither am I arguing that professionals trained in the sciences, business, or engineering fall under a 'false consciousness' of technocratic complicity without the capacity for self-reflection. As Hasan (2021) has noted in his work on rural bureaucracy and mobile apps, the contribution of engineers to local bureaucracies can indeed bring in fresh perspectives and creatively address gaps between citizens, bureaucrats, and representatives. Indeed, my focus is more on white-collar technocrats steeped in corporate professionalism who work in the fields of policy and management consulting, rather than simply those who have training and proficiency in the sciences, engineering, and technology. Most importantly, I am investigating a structural shift: how a subset of technocrats and/or professionals who follow a particular trajectory of education and professional training are being given greater control over processes of top-down governance. An increased outsourcing to these professionals has significant implications for the elite insularity of policymaking, its distance from political plurality, and, as such, democratic representation.

Conceptualising the Markets

The policy market has been growing since the early 2000s, while the election market began to snowball in 2012. Over the last five to ten years, the infrastructure of both markets has been rapidly populating with more organisations that sell ideas and expertise, competing with one another for political and policy influence. I conceptualise participants in the *policy market* to consist of global consulting firms, think tanks, business lobbies, chambers of commerce, and policy research organisations. The market consists of the transactions between these sellers and government agencies. While global consulting firms have been working on government projects in India since the early 2000s, the last five years have seen a rapid growth in their involvement. At the same time, policy schools, engineering schools, and business schools have begun to specifically educate graduates to cater to this market. The *election market*, on the other hand, gained national attention primarily during Prime Minister Modi's campaign leading up to the 2014 national election. Crucially, Modi's campaigns to run for chief minister in Gujarat in the 2000s were also a precursor of the professionalisation of politics. Consultants began to be hired as agents of political persuasion by political parties, calling on tools of increasing global relevance: data mining and micro-targeting (mis)information to drastically change the everyday practices of politics.

While the two markets function through separate networks that sell distinct ideas and strategies, they are connected through a world view of 'creative but pragmatic' problem-solving. A technocratic discourse that argues that it is those outside the dregs of a corrupt politics and stagnant bureaucracy who know best is revived here, yet those who are considered authoritative experts have changed. The outsiders who are hired to run the democratic process are increasingly the managers, engineers, and commerce, finance, and business graduates: a particular kind of 'professional'.

When political parties hire such professionals to target election campaigns, mine private data, and potentially manipulate voters, how does this influence the production of political promises made to an electorate? When voters then elect representatives who hire external professionals to make policy, how does that affect diverse representation in government? Such emerging forms of inwardness can exacerbate elite confidentiality around vital decisions about politics and society, which only deepen the long-existing chasm between governance and popular consciousness in India. While there is ostensibly competition between firms in both the election market and the policy market, the self-professed ideological principles that guide these firms are largely similar: to fix corrupt politics and broken governance through increased efficiency and privatisation.

Technocratic professionals and management consultants often see their increased influence as deepening democratic participation. In June 2019, I spoke to the political consultant known to many as having 'revolutionised election campaigning' in India: Prashant Kishor. Kishor has built an institutional model that sees professionals in democracy as able to combine 'professional' processes (i.e. technological efficiency and strategic planning) with modes of representative democracy. However, he explained his desire to distance himself from dominant conceptions of global political consulting, saying 'the participation of professionals in democracy, especially in electoral politics in India is different from political consultancies in the West'.[1]

---

[1] Kishor's stated desire to bring professionals into democracy potentially unsettles Chatterjee's distinction between civil society and political society. As mentioned in an earlier footnote, Chatterjee's (2008) distinction between political society and civil society addresses the differential routes the modern-corporate class (civil society – through civic organisations, influence, and pressure) and working-informal class (political society – through negotiations and electoral democratic means) must take in order to make demands from the state in post-colonial India. Kishor's words suggest the possibility for the modern-corporate class to engage in political society in order to expand civic political participation for this class.

Here, Kishor implied a key distinction between professionals in India 'deepening' civic participation, and political consultancies in the West 'stifling' democracy through data mining and manipulative targeting (i.e. Cambridge Analytica).

The validity of this claim is debatable. The effect that a growth of consultants has on the quality of democracy depends, in large part, on what kind of normative choice we make about democratic quality. Literature on policy studies often oscillates between the dominant model of a liberal, representative democracy (what Barber (1984) calls a 'thin' democracy); a participatory democracy (a 'strong' democracy); or an issue-based combination of the two (Fischer 2004). Scholars have argued that the professionalising of democratic processes tends to conflate liberal conceptions of representative democracy with dominant notions of technical expertise: advocating for bypassing political procedure in favour of having the state hire professionals (Negrine et al. 2007). The participation of professionals in democracy, as Kishor says, is understood to improve civic confidence and engagement in an otherwise defunct political system. Professionals who distance themselves from politics see themselves as post-ideological and able to 'fix' the system, while remaining unencumbered by irrational partisanship. Because of the relatively recent development of these trends, it is difficult to claim tangible implications of these changes for democracy. However, this outsourcing and the production of 'rationality' in politics and governance builds a professional industry that reproduces a singular (and often anti-political) conception of 'common good'. In the process, it obfuscates (and silences) the power struggles inherent in political plurality and procedural legitimacy (Bickerton and Accetti 2017).

Think tanks and policy research organisations have some semblance of academic, government, or industry credibility and experience. They consist of former or current government bureaucrats, businessmen, politicians, researchers qualified (mostly) with PhDs, academics, retired military personnel, Members of Parliament, and prominent journalists. Consulting firms tend to house primarily technical professionals – graduates from science, engineering, finance, policy, and management schools with work experience in banks, IT companies, multinational corporations, and mainstream business consulting firms. These professionals focus on data analysis and solutions to policy implementation challenges, working with governments and political parties as 'clients'. Along with working for political and management consulting firms, several of these graduates also tend to join chambers of commerce, political parties, and think tanks in different capacities with different professional roles. However, it is primarily the consulting firms in these markets that make the most effort at recruiting from technical or management training institutes.

POLICY MARKET

Bureaucracy: From Managing to Outsourcing

In the realm of policymaking, canonical sociological theories of governance have been grounded in 'rational-legal' theories of bureaucracy. Classical sociological texts on bureaucratisation emphasise the superior forms of efficiency and depersonalisation of bureaucratic systems (Weber 1958) and, as such, the rationalisation inherent to its structural violence: enumeration, categorisation, recording, and depoliticising inscription (as an 'iron cage' (Weber 1958)). Along similar lines, though, through a more subversive critique, Foucault (2008) saw bureaucratic and administrative structures shaping human existence in far more intimate ways: through 'an explosion of numerous and diverse techniques for achieving the subjugation of bodies and the control of populations'.

Empirical studies of bureaucracy have gradually shifted from characterising state bureaucracies as agents of immense efficiency and administrative control of human existence, to, more recently, as disjointed and blundering in performance (Etzioni-Halevy 2013). As Akhil Gupta's critical study of the Indian state shows, scholars have focused on the inefficiency and indifference of the bureaucracy to respond to the distinct and varied welfare needs of a diversely impoverished population (Gupta 2012). Another genre of literature on bureaucracies studies the discourse of anti-bureaucratic fervour: as Herzfeld evocatively notes, 'if one could not grumble about "bureaucracy", bureaucracy itself could not easily exist: both bureaucracy and the stereotypical complaints about it are parts of a larger universe that we might call the ideology and the practice of accountability' (Herzfeld 1993, 2). This discourse of grumbling about the stagnancy of bureaucracy and a general lack of accountability has partially lent strength to the growth of 'managerialism' in the state: bringing corporate managers into governance.

'Managerialism' is understood through a variety of characteristics: as a managerial class that commands organisations but does not own them; as managers who serve 'controllers of capital' by controlling labourers (Sivaramakrishnan 2012, 1); and as possessing a universally applicable technical expertise (Grey 1999). Common to all these definitions is understanding managerialism as a distinctive elite that possesses universalist knowledge to 'deploy calculative power' (Clarke and Newman 1997, 66). Through a growing mainstreaming of corporate styles of management in the 1980s, managerialism slowly injected itself into state bureaucracy: both as an ideology and as state practice (Saint-Martin 2004). A 'New' Managerialism emerged globally through the Thatcher and Reagan years (Davies 2003) as part of an ideology committed to reshaping unfit public sector institutions, including the civil services. As well as representing a belief that the market should dictate the means of resource allocation and thus that the state needs managers to 'manage' this transformation, the entry of external management into governance had a distinct effect on governance. As Clarke and Newman (1997) note, managerialism was seen as rigorously disciplined and businesslike: a driving force for productivity, efficiency, and a progressive social force.

In India, the Planning Commission, consisting of bureaucrats, technocrats, economists, and industrialists, was set up post-Independence to oversee state planning and allocate budgets to further industrial development and social development. The loosening of trade restrictions in computer products in the 1980s did modernise some public administration services, such as railways and banking, yet the sophisticated data analysis and technological modernisation key to managerialism had not yet penetrated deeply entrenched conceptions of policy and political decision-making. Liberalisation of the economy in 1991 furthered foreign and private participation in the economy, paving the path for private expertise to gain greater value in the public domain (Corbridge and Harriss 2013). Kaviraj (2010a) argues that the changes spurred by liberalisation were not merely 'technical' (2010b, 240). Rather, though the apparent economic vision of liberalisation was meant to reduce the state's economic role, it required a significant use of political power to manifest itself, particularly as it worked in favour of the country's urban, industrial, and agricultural elites. The self-interested individual as an 'economic' individual gained strength as a cultural construct, increasing legitimacy for private capital accumulation, and the continued failure of the state to invest in education, health, and social programmes. Over the last three decades, this has given rise to an aspirational 'home-grown' technocracy that allies itself with capitalist endeavour and economic growth through paradigms of private business and a sturdy state–business alliance. It furthered what Paula Chakravartty (2004) termed 'techno-populism', a combination of technology and populism: state-driven projects to 'outfit the masses with technology' (Irani 2019, 38), which came to be infused with the idea of novelty and innovation as a unique force for national growth.

The growth of managerialism has led management consultants to play a more significant role in Indian public sector projects and policy formulation. In the early to mid-2000s, Leftist political parties challenged the inclusion of private and foreign consulting firms in the government's Planning Commission (Ramachandran 2004). An interview with a former chairman for BCG India describes this transition:

In the early 2000s, consulting firms were not consulting with the government. That was when Rajat Gupta established McKinsey Global Institute – in India it was very new to use that platform to engage with policymaking. Yet it was dismissed as pure management, with people saying that [management consultants] don't understand the complexities. In the government in 2004, the Deputy Chairman of the Planning Commission had decided to bring consulting firms to various consultative bodies to do a midterm appraisal. Within a week of these forums meeting, the [Left] objected, saying that it's immoral to get foreign consultants into advisor roles. All the other consultants promptly resigned, and didn't want to take embarrassment further ... But you see, what the [Leftist] chap said, I mean he had a point. They [consulting firms] build a point of view that they're known for, and they want that point of view to be present, that's their own ideology.

(Interview with a former chairman of BCG India, July 2019)

Since 2004, growing attitudes towards the bureaucracy as stagnant, corrupt, and inadequate have given rise to support for outsourcing government projects to private consultants outside of government administration. This outsourcing echoes Von Mises' 1944 treatise on bureaucratic systems as a detriment to progress, 'what must be realised is only that the strait jacket of bureaucratic organisation paralyses the individual's initiative, while within the capitalist market society an innovator still has a chance to succeed' (Von Mises and Greaves 1944, 124) . An interview with a high-ranking bureaucrat in charge of one of the ruling party's flagship schemes notes, in a similar vein, that there needs to be greater participation of the private sector in government programmes:

There's definitely greater participation of the private sector in public service delivery [since 2014]. I mean, it's not at a desirable state, because the government has a fundamental distrust of the private sector. Till we actually opened up the economy in 1991, private was [a] strict no no, we had to have everything in the public domain. We had a public sector enterprise for every possible product or service that we wanted, from telecom to hotels to bread to aviation parts to ... there was no concept of ever calling a private sector guy and either seeking his input or asking them to do something. But now things are very different. In fact, just a couple of days back they allowed some lateral entries.

(Interview with a high-ranking bureaucrat in the Indian Administrative Services, March 2019)

The 'lateral entry' pathway is tied into this shift. Thus far, the path to enter the Indian Administrative Services (apart from a few exceptions) has been a highly competitive nationwide examination, followed by intense shortlisting and interview processes. In 2019, the Indian government allowed nine corporate professionals and technical experts to move into the civil services through 'lateral entry'. Despite criticism that this process has the potential to be 'greatly misused' by bringing in 'political appointees' (i.e. people favoured by the ruling political party), many public intellectuals and analysts have supported it, arguing that the Indian government cadres are in great need of 'fresh talent'.

The conversation about lateral entry into the IAS has been a long one, with the demand being featured repeatedly in BJP's 2014 manifesto. Rajendra Pratap Gupta, one of the key drafters of the BJP manifesto (Gupta 2019), wrote in a national newspaper that Indian bureaucratic officers at higher levels of administrative power have mostly been composed of elite members of society or caste-based affirmative action recruits (Mandal 2019). Allowing for lateral entry into government, in his view, allows for the dissolution of this elite and/or 'undeserved' hold over governance. However, this move primarily replaces an old form of bureaucratic elite with a new, seemingly 'meritocratic' professional elite. Here, the corporate professional as the government outsider is considered more businesslike, more skilled, and more deserving of a role in the Indian Administrative Services. Indeed, the 'seductiveness' (Thompson 2016, 94) of new managerialism is in its language of empowerment, accountability, and client-centric transparency. The same high-ranking bureaucrat explains that the increased participation of consulting firms in government ministries allows the government to benefit from their 'talent':

> Nine joint secretaries were inducted into the government on contract basis. And it's a great start obviously. It's good that, you know, subject matter experts come and share what is to be done . . . And without actually getting these experts as officers in government, you [still] have their talent pool available – now you have all the big consulting houses working in all [the] critical paths of government. We have a team of 15 consultants from PricewaterhouseCoopers. And similarly, all major schemes are being supported by Deloitte or Accenture, PwC and McKinsey. It's entrenched.
>
> *(Interview with a high-ranking bureaucrat in the*
> *Indian Administrative Services, March 2019)*

Yet management consultants do little to recalibrate faulty delivery systems or policy aims. They may bring more efficient systems of capturing data and monitoring actors in top-down systems, yet, as development economist Lant Pritchett has argued, these often track only 'thin' indicators of change (Honig and Pritchett 2019). For example, assessing whether schools are teaching their students the skills and competencies to succeed are reduced to 'thin' input-based indicators like textbook availability, enrolment numbers, and class sizes, rather than more substantive, 'thick' decentralised metrics that take into account the experiences of frontline agents and difficult-to-codify local knowledges (Honig and Pritchett 2019).

Entrenched but Concealed

While the involvement of private consultants has been made evident, the extent of their influence is undocumented. In the summer of 2019, I filed several Right to Information (the Indian equivalent of the US Freedom of Information Act) requests to the Home Ministry, the

Finance Ministry, and the NITI Aayog (the government's primary think tank) requesting data on the hiring of external consulting firms on government projects over the last decade. These requests proved futile, with responses directing me to public data released by the Ministry of Planning that vaguely measured the amount spent on 'professional services'. While 'professional services' can include most external services, it allows us to map a general change over time: the budget increased fivefold between 2016–2017 and 2017–2018, and rose by 30 per cent in 2018–2019. Turnover at Indian consulting firms grew by an average of 10.8 per cent annually in the five years up to 2018, according to Euromonitor, with industry revenues in India totalling $64.8 billion that year (Shrikanth 2019) (this measurement includes contracts with private industry and government). A major reason why exact data proved difficult to access is that prominent global consulting firms have made their way into Indian government projects primarily over the last ten years (according to interviews with senior partners at Ernst & Young and PricewaterhouseCoopers) and tend to evade publicising their involvement.

The 'influence', per se, of such firms, exists at two levels: first, they are advisor consultants hired by government ministries to provide input on certain projects/schemes/strategy. As a senior partner and leader of government and public sector projects at a global consulting firm in India told me:

> We are doing a lot of work with the Government of India, we're working with 24 central ministries now, 25 state governments, in some shape or fashion. Since we are there, we get good insights into what whole departments or ministries are doing. Leading out of that, even if it's not our role, we will take it – look at it carefully – look at some benchmarks from around the world and flush that back into this system at the Secretary level, or the Minister level. And if they like it, then they can sponsor us to do more work. So that's another conduit.
>
> *(Interview with senior partner and leader of government and public sector projects at a global consulting firm, July 2019)*

Here, the emphasis on global best practices ('benchmarks from around the world') gestures towards another key discourse surrounding the necessity and inevitability of consulting firms working within government: the competitive positioning of nations in the global economy. The Indian government's growing political assertion of its prominence on the global economic stage promises its credibility to compete in a global marketplace with the help of multinational consulting firms. As such, reports from McKinsey, Ernst & Young, and similar firms lend the country 'validation', making it appear an attractive destination for foreign investors (Choudhury and Sinha 2004).

The second form of influence is through the public relations machinery of these companies that allows specific individuals to emerge as 'thought leaders' in particular sectors, with expertise in those sectors. Adil Zainulbhai, former chairman of McKinsey India, was hired as the head of the Quality Council of India, an organisation that functions as the national industrial accreditation board. Amber Dubey from KPMG has become known in public discourse as an expert in aerospace engineering and, as such, has become one of the nine lateral entry officers inducted by the government. A key attribute of the marketisation of the policy market is that the influence of these particular firms is never publicly known, yet acknowledged primarily in 'slide decks' presented to potential clients to demonstrate market credibility. The lines between advocacy, advice, and lobbying here are blurry. While checks and balances exist within these firms to prevent lobbying, it is purposefully hard to trace where certain recommendations emerge from. A senior partner at one of the major consulting firms in India emphasises this 'informal' influence over policy and politics, from working on political party manifestos to determining policy visions for the next five years:

> Some [consulting firms] are just doing operation consulting, project design, project management, and project implementation. But the McKinseys and BCGs and Ernst & Young definitely work in the

policy field and we work at multiple levels – on policy because there are multiple stakeholders, not one stakeholder, we will work with political parties in getting them to understand potentially what could go into their manifesto. A lot of that consultation is informal. And sometimes, it is formalised through a project with the state government's planning department. Because you know – for example – six to eight months before the elections, we will be asked, or we are already working with the planning departments, on, you know, what should be the vision for the next five years.

(Interview with senior partner and leader of government and public sector projects at a global consulting firm, July 2019)

The interviewee expresses, along with his firm's participation in determining policy imperatives, a blurring of the election market and the policy market. The central dilemma here rests at the heart of notions of representative democracy and private expertise. The moral universe of those invested in the technocratic consensus – whether this includes professionals, managers, executives, or consultants – affirms that they are indispensable to success. In this story, overcoming the irrationality of political play and stagnant bureaucracy requires their capacity to grasp complexity, manage well, and reap its rewards. As such, the imperatives and fortunes of the individual manager, the firm, and the nation are linked (Clarke and Newman 1997, 66). New managerialism offers itself as the antithesis of the old bureau professional, the inert and complacent IAS officer in the Indian bureaucratic treadmill.

Training the Next Generation of Policy Professionals

The infrastructure of sustaining this pipeline of professionals into the policy market relies on the creation of specific public policy training institutes. Since 2014, major private and public universities such as the Indian Institute of Management, the Indian School of Business, and the Jindal Institute of Government and Public Policy, to name a few, have instituted dedicated public policy and governance

programmes, degrees, and training certificates. In 2019, a new institute called the Indian School of Public Policy (ISPP) was launched in
New Delhi, using a training curriculum to teach the 'management of
institutions of governance' to its students. The ISPP has made claims
to securing partnerships with massive 'industry leaders' including
Deloitte, Uber, PricewaterhouseCoopers, Twitter, Skill India,
Confederation of Indian Industry, amongst others. These corporations
are partnered with ISPP to build a training curriculum and 'cultivate
networks of professional participation', even boasting training
through a 'policy hackathon' ('ISPP' 2019). An interview on the necessity of the institute with a founding member of ISPP revealed:

> Much of the work is done by consultants. If you look at the
> Ministry of Human Resource Development, the staff is PwC or
> KPMG guys who are sitting and doing much of the work. They
> don't have policy backgrounds, most of them are MBAs, almost all
> of them. So they're going to be hired anyway, and be paid by the
> government in pretty good sums. So if KPMG had at least some
> policy graduates in their team, they might do a better job in
> advising governments about what they're doing.
>
> *(Interview with head of a think tank and the founder of*
> *Indian School of Public Policy, March 2019)*

This, however, brings up the question of what consultants are trained
to do. An interview with a current advisor at a major global consulting
firm in India tells me that, primarily, these skills lie in the 'framing' of
an issue. The epistemological work at play here becomes about
framing issues, policy challenges, and, thus, policy priorities.

> I've come into meetings where BCG teams who know nothing
> about this subject are advising teams of Ministers. But they've got
> the best that consultants give. When you put young people who go
> out and get a lot of information, they digest it and put it out. That's
> where their competencies lay. And that's where the problem is, you
> see. We'll do a global search of best practices, we'll offer to do

20 countries. Then we'll do so many interviews in those countries and research, then you tick the boxes to say this was done, and then present it. When you frame the problem in a certain way, you frame the research question to suit both of them, the government and the consultant. So you have to ask, what is the value of this to the government? What does it take to change the system? In India – if the knowledge you bring in from a large consulting company is already framed through a particular point of view, for a purpose – what value are you adding?

(Interview with a current advisor at a major global consulting firm in India, August 2019)

Several key themes I have introduced so far are enacted by this interviewee. Here, the 'problem' to be fixed is determined by consultants prior to its investigation, as are the particular technical and political categories within it. These defined categories emerge from an existing framework of 'thin' accountability (Honig and Pritchett 2019) best practices, reconstituted by consulting firms that sell their expertise to government projects. The specificities of substantive knowledge that politicians and civil servants might have from many years of working in a field is disregarded in favour of a superficial, universalist policy prescription. As Honig and Pritchett (2019) argue in the context of RCT trials in Indian educational reforms, 'We believe the devil is not in the details of the intervention, but rather in the theory of change upon which it is premised – in the belief that technology driven interventions [that prioritise context-free, quantifiable metrics] are a promising route to systems improvement' (Honig and Pritchett 2019, 3).

Winch's (2008) example of a monk's life is a useful parallel here: one might be able to describe the daily tasks of a monk and give an account of his relations with other monks and people outside the monastery, yet without a deeper understanding of the substantive religious ideals that guide these actions, the description remains unintelligible. Indeed, without substantively engaging with long-term practitioners' activities and attributing an agential sense of internal motivation to them, it becomes difficult to ascertain why they do what they do: their intentions, mistakes, unintended consequences, and justifications for their actions. In imposing a universalist solution to varied governance challenges, the consultant enacts a fundamental folly of managerialism: reducing a plurality of motivations and experiences within governance to a limited range of thin, quantifiable metrics (Sivaramakrishnan 2012).

ELECTION MARKET: 'IDEOLOGICALLY AGNOSTIC'

Electoral Processes in Democracy

The desire to heighten technocratic decision-making in policy is often seen as a counter to the irrational nature of political partisanship, self-interest, 'soft' metrics of performance, and corruption within bureaucratic and political systems. In tandem, an effort to bring order to a messy and corrupt political system has ushered in a new market of political consulting firms. Political consultants come from the same pool as management consultants and similarly eschew ideological partisanship in favour of an agnostic notion of civic participation in democracy. In this section, I suggest that the 'ideologically agnostic' nature of political consultants' professional expertise powers a discourse that deepens the increasingly widening fissure between politics, representative governance, and political participation. While they see themselves in favour of a form of public good that is anti-political (Ferguson 1994), I argue that their increasing involvement is diminishing democratic plurality. Indeed, in campaigning for what they call a 'stable and good' governance structure, they tend to work for the political party with the greatest access to electoral funds, often the same parties aligned with significant corporate interests. The allusion to 'stable and good', then, gestures to notions of public good emerging from stable economic markets.

The democratic process is, ideally, about more than just elections (Malleson 2018). Classical political theorists (Hallas 1983; Springborg 1984), as well as Indian subaltern scholars (Chatterjee

2011), argue that discourses of universal suffrage in democracies often tend to falsely homogenise differential political power amongst citizens ('one person, one vote'). This can have the tendency to conceal silenced voices and diverse forms of economic and structural violence experienced by marginalised groups in deeply unequal societies. Yet those who are voted into power have a strong hand in shaping democratic processes. Electing political representation, then, is the cornerstone of a representative democracy, and the liberal democratic process also claims to account for minority protection, constitutional rule of law, checks and balances, and the accountable dispersal of power.

Globally, the profession of advertising political clients predates even corporate advertising. Political consulting can be traced in other parts of the world as far back as the 1930s and much has been written on political consulting in the United States (Cain 2011; Johnson 2016; Medvic 2003; Sheingate 2016), countries in Europe (Karlsen 2010; Strömbäck 2009), and recent democracies (Lisi 2013). In the United States, Baxter and Whitaker started *Campaigns Inc.*, spearheading the use of advertising techniques for political campaigning and pioneering new methods of persuasion through targeted messaging, pamphleting, and narrativising (Sheingate 2016). They 'forged a lucrative business *of* politics by discovering new ways to organise business *in* politics' (Sheingate 2016, 9). Over the next several decades, Madison Avenue advertising professionals participated in a few presidential campaigns, yet it took until the 1980s for the term 'political consultant' to be considered a full-fledged, profitable business (Johnson 2016). Whether Indian political parties campaign on the basis of ideologically coherent platforms or a coalition-centric compromise of promises is a longrunning debate (Chhibber and Verma 2018). Regardless, consultants' growing control over election campaigns and popular political visions widens the extant gap between elite leadership and popular consciousness.

Political consultants work with parties to win elections. Professionalising this process can refer to a number of activities, but particularly to the creation of a more 'rational' (Negrine et al. 2007) and streamlined political organisational structure. This can mean better use of demographic data to help with targeting voters, skilful uses of forms of communication, and the reorganisation of political parties themselves. Crucially, however, the process of professionalising political parties and elections aims to enact a 'rationalisation of persuasion' (Mayhew 1997, 189). Here, the rationalisation of persuasion refers to the process of producing a product (i.e. campaign) that is better for consumption. In turn, if the product fails to 'sell well', the lead actors (i.e. the key politicians) or the programme itself (the party's election promises) must be changed. While reports on the growing influence of political consulting in India argue that the tactics of persuasion have only been magnified, I suggest that these perceived changes are not neutral. Rather, they have been amplified beyond measure through the use of more specific, efficient, and widespread databases and technological expertise. This amplification comes with new forms of identifying, targeting, and defining issues of political importance. Indeed, in interpreting, recreating, and reproducing the allegiances of the candidate as well as individual voters, consultants have the power to 'create the very context in which they work' (Sheingate 2016, 10). An interview with a tech journalist revealed the growing reliance on data analytics in the election market:

> This is the Moneyball moment of politics, especially data analytics. There was this time you could use statistics in baseball games to figure out statistics. This introduction of data into electoral strategies is something that professionals have the ability to do, which is not something you expect from a political party worker – you may have context, but not the ability to write computer programs and to mine data. One of the few things would be that you can create booth level, constituency level profiles, demographic profiles, figure out caste, positions – figure out what your chances are.

As this interview excerpt explains, the key difference between a long-time party worker and a professional is that the professional consultant is able to build data sets, compile demographic data, and strategise political campaigns in a systematic way – one that works through rational calculation of the 'odds' of winning.

> You can channel your energy better if you have a micro-level understanding of a constituency, add it to a state, then add it to the national-level – whatever domain you're fighting your election in, you can accordingly think about messaging, issues, all that. It's good, especially if you're fighting a close election. Doing an election well is about margins – if there are two lakh people in a constituency and you can manage to shift twenty thousand people – it matters. It's huge. This whole idea of thinking very statistically about election strategy – I think that's a very distinct area where professionalisation matters.
>
> *(Interview with a tech journalist, March 2019)*

With India's first-past-the-post system,[2] influencing ambivalent voters matters. But to what extent does campaigning change minds? Sachin Rao, the man in charge of training party workers within the Congress Party, notes that elections are not won through the campaigns that take place over the months leading up to the elections, but rather over the four years of the ruling party's performance. This analysis, while supported by studies on the minimal 'campaign-effect' of election outcomes (Kalla and Broockman 2018), fails to address how targeted narratives can capitalise on material realities, shaping how voters relate to their leaders and make sense of their circumstances (Bonikowski 2017). The degree of persuadability varies according to levels of 'affective polarisation' that make citizens more or less susceptible to persistent framing devices (Iyengar et al. 2012). I do not argue that campaign strategists can become kingmakers. Rather, I gesture to the deep democratic implications of outsourcing elections

---

[2] India's Constitution adopts a first-past-the-post system in which a candidate who receives the greatest number of votes wins the seat in a particular constituency. This is used in India in direct elections to the Lok Sabha (Lower House of Parliament) and State Legislative Assembly, and has been key to the BJP's rise.

to a mass of professional consultants, and the discourse that sustains their industry.

Scholarship on political persuasion in Indian elections highlights the clientelism evident in local and regional elections (Das and Maiorano 2019), the capturing of 'vote banks' through strategic promises (Chauchard 2018), and handouts in interest-group politics (Elliott 2011). Political consulting firms see their work as bringing order to the corruption and 'messiness' of Indian politics. While their involvement follows the logic of technocratic outsourcing, much of their tactics, technologies, and processes are new. Older parties like the BJP often have a strong and geographically diverse structure of disciplined party workers. The BJP's foot soldiers, for example, include the seven-decade-long paramilitary organisation, the RSS, that can access remote parts of the country to build loyalty and support for the party. Yet political consultants target voters and constituencies in different ways: while they work closely with the political party to develop content that supports the party's messaging, they formulate new messages and election promises that will resonate with voters. In some cases, they use their demographic data to decide who should run from a constituency to maximise their chance of winning. As such, they play integral roles both in formulating political content and targeting it to maximum effect.

In 2012, the Samajwadi Party in Uttar Pradesh, for example, heavily relied on professional consultants to direct its campaign. Prior to 2012, political parties had only occasionally hired external advertising agencies to create large-scale campaigns highlighting the party, instead of engaging with voters to target messages. While Prime Minister Rajiv Gandhi relied on white-collar professionals, technological tools, and rigorous data analysis during his tenure in the 1980s, political parties did not appreciate techno-managerialism as an electioneering tool until more recently (Sharma 2022). In 1989, the Congress Party hired Rediffusion, an Indian advertising agency, to run an unsuccessful campaign ('My Heart Beats for India'). In 2004, the BJP hired Grey Worldwide, an international advertising agency (who also worked with Samsung and Hyundai), to run their (also unsuccessful) 'India Shining' campaign. The employment of professional data analysts and strategists in this process, however, has been a recent but quickly growing development with significant implications for Indian electioneering. First, it both specifies voters of interest and targets messaging on a much larger scale. Second, it introduces an apolitical and 'ideologically agnostic' approach to backroom political strategy that has, thus far, been driven by political partisanship, grassroots loyalty, clientelism, familiality, and/or ideological positioning. Indeed, it is the apparent political 'neutrality' of these backroom consultants that gives them the credibility to work with several competing political parties, seemingly without self-interest and thus considered trustworthy. Third, it brings technocratic professionalism into the electoral process to an unprecedented degree, turning election campaigns into an established and profitable market. Some parties thus have more funds to access finely tuned campaign strategies that could narrow the parties that are able to effectively participate in a multiparty system.

As more techniques become available in the areas of business and commerce, such as marketing strategy, news media management, and advertising, the professionalisation of commercial skills becomes more and more applicable to political communication (Negrine et al. 2007). As Mayhew (1997) notes, new scientific methods can also lead to new campaigning techniques (i.e. the use of polling was predicated on improvements in sampling methods). In India, approximately 64 per cent of the population is reported to have mobile phones (Pew Research Center 2019) and over 40 per cent has an internet subscription and more data for cheaper rates (data costs have dropped by 95 per cent since 2013 (McKinsey Global Institute 2019)), ensuring that a growing segment of Indians uses social media. A former consultant at Indian Political Action Committee (IPAC) and Jarvis Consulting (an offshoot of IPAC) explains the impact that new mediums of communication can have on political persuasion and election campaigning.

As far as strategizing, it has given us more avenues we can use. The way of communication has expanded since PM Modi's campaign in 2014. The usage of social media was there before that but people have started having separate social media cells, small parties have social media units, all candidates have their social media teams. Because they know to spread the word amongst the youth which is more available online, it is really needed to connect with them through that medium.

(Interview with former consultant at IPAC and Jarvis Consulting, June 2019)

While amplification allows messages to be targeted and delivered in more widespread ways, this former consultant gestures to another key dimension to this form of communication: it combines mass appeal with personal connection.

Social media has opened a lot of avenues but the core things are the same. Even today, the politicians we meet have the same things in mind, they want to connect with the people, want to tell them what's in the manifesto and what they have to offer. The only thing is with technical advances they can easily reach the masses and don't have to fly to their constituencies all the time to deliver the same messages.

(Interview with former consultant at IPAC and Jarvis Consulting, June 2019)

Politicians and political parties can connect more directly with their constituents through WhatsApp groups and Facebook messages. They can send individually tailored messages to a person's phone, WhatsApp account, or Facebook account, accessing their psyche in a more private way. The crisis of Cambridge Analytica has revealed the risks of melding technological prowess and data mining with strategies of political persuasion. Facebook and WhatsApp in India have faced criticism for giving way to political parties' campaigning strategies, spreading misinformation and building highly targeted algorithms of knowledge dispersal. Indeed, the former Head of Public

Policy at WhatsApp India was previously working for a BJP IT cell, formulating strategies to build support for the party. These networks run deep, turning the practical work of elections into a data-driven, technologically oriented, thriving business with far-reaching implications.

The Consultants

Since 2014, the mechanisms of national election campaigns in India are being gradually handed over to political consultants: young graduates of the sciences, technology, engineering, and management fields, who use data mining and strategic technological targeting to, effectively, tell voters what they want to hear. Foot soldiers, cadres, and on-the-ground party workers continue to do the work they do in a traditional party structure, but are increasingly being directed by young professionals working as political consultants who gain their legitimacy from top party leadership. As a LinkedIn job advertisement posted for Jarvis Consulting declares:

> As a group of young Indians, our dream is to bring about a positive change in our country's socio-political scenario with a goal to see India become a developed country. Jarvis is committed to leveraging technology and research to plug the informational, structural and operational inefficiencies in the fields of politics and governance. We are on track to become the largest tech-focused strategy consulting firm in these areas.
>
> *(LinkedIn, Job advertisement posted for Jarvis Consulting, a BJP political consulting firm)*

Political consulting firms have been hired by political parties on a smaller scale, for individual politicians and state elections, over the last few decades – from image management companies to boutique strategic consulting firms, to larger global firms such as Strategic Consulting Ltd. (which also owns Cambridge Analytica). The 2014 national election, however, introduced political consultants in Indian national politics. The IPAC, founded by Prashant Kishor, is one of the key political consulting firms hired by parties fighting both national- and state-level elections. Along with IPAC, other significant firms include offshoots started by former IPAC employees, such as Jarvis Consulting and Association for a Billion Minds (ABM).

The industry body Assocham counted 150 firms in 2014 that referred to themselves as political consultants. By the 2014 national election, the industry was reported to be worth $40–$47 million in annual revenue (Sinha 2014). Between 2014 and 2018, industry specialists estimate that the number of firms in this market had at least doubled. A typology of political consulting firms active in this growing professional arena varies according to their scale and association with specific political parties. As a journalist working on an investigative study of ABM explained, some are housed inside a political party, while others are not loyal to a party but move between them ('the IPAC model, where you're not loyal to a particular party – now they're with Mamata Banerjee. They've done work with Congress, RJD, and Prashant Kishor rose with the BJP'). Others work with individual politicians. While industry-wide data is difficult to access and has yet to be systematically measured, the scale of operations is multiplying: Political Edge, a boutique consulting firm, has worked on average for 100 candidates a year since it started in 2011 (Sarkar n.d.). WarRoom Strategies, a consulting firm founded in 2016, expanded from 40 employees to 700 in just two years.

IPAC's roots can be traced back to another organisation started by Prashant Kishor called the Citizens for Accountable Governance (CAG), which gained strength through working on Prime Minister Modi's 2014 election campaign. Initially a public health expert, he reportedly saw himself as ideologically agnostic (Thakur 2016) – not attached to a particular political credo, but rather to tangible and pragmatic policy solutions. The run-up to the 2014 national elections inspired many young professionals to place hope in a new government to challenge the reigning Congress Party, and a desire to drive political change – yet, crucially, not *through* politics. Instead, Kishor started CAG and hired young graduates from the Indian Institute of

Technology (IIT) and Indian Institute of Management (IIM) with the offer to direct change through their strategic, creative, and technological skills. Kishor and the CAG team managed Modi's political campaign – the first of its kind – introducing a candidate-focused mode of campaigning. As a key member of Modi's strategic team, Kishor planned several of his most spectacular campaign highlights, including the *chai pe charcha*, 3D rallies, and a 'unity run', while harnessing the role of social media armies to campaign for the BJP (Chaturvedi 2016). Before Modi's overwhelming win, Kishor was promised a key advisory role in infrastructure and development with the new government (Thakur 2016). However, according to a former CAG employee, he was reportedly dismissed by the BJP's leadership and not given the key policy role he was hoping for:

> At the time [Modi] was coming to power, he may have promised something [to Kishor], but was apparently taking a lot of time with it. And then Modi said, 'Okay, well, you said you're professionals – you can carry on with your work.' Those were his exact words. He was like 'Well, you're professionals. What, have you come with a new presentation?' He actually said, '*Jab shaadi hoti hai, toh sab log aate hain, tent log aate hain, caterers aate hain* [when there's a wedding, all the people come, the tent people come, the caterers come], and once the couple is married, everyone goes back to their lives. So *shaadi khatam ho gayi* [the wedding is over], and you said you're professionals, so I guess you can go back to doing what you're doing'.
>
> *(Interview with former CAG employee, June 2019)*

This moment reinforces the notion that political consultants gain their professional legitimacy by staying 'out of' politics. Prashant Kishor's desire to be a part of the government is an outlier, as the majority of political consultants gain market credibility from being able to mould their campaigns according to different political parties' messages, whether these messages are straightforwardly 'ideological' (as in the case of Hindu supremacy with the BJP) or opportunistic election promises that will most appeal to voters. The end of Modi's campaign led to the dissolution of CAG into two separate organisations: IPAC and the Citizen's Alliance. Since 2016, IPAC has paved the path for several more influential political consulting firms, and expanded from 50 to 60 employees in 2016 to more than 600 in 2019.[3]

Political consultants tend to be engineering, science, and management graduates from the country's top-most universities, who enter the field for a variety of reasons – most significantly because of their social networks. Graduates are recruited by alumni of their university, whom they implicitly trust. This work appeals to young professionals for one of two reasons: first, offering involvement in the election campaign to bring 'change' and help bring about a vaguely 'good, stable' government; and second, a fast-paced, exciting work environment promised to them by former students of their institution. These two motivations have one key attribute in common: they proclaim and reveal themselves as 'post'-ideology, and use that as their strength. This is premised on the idea that the existing state and bureaucratic structure is stagnant and inefficient, and that politics, while deeply influential, is a corrupt farce. A current political consultant highlights this approach towards 'ideological politics' in the following quotation:

> I personally do not believe in the concept of ideology, I don't think any party, except maybe a hard-core Hindutva BJP … many Indian parties don't have a hard-core ideology. From election to election they're changing the ideas they're putting in front of the possible voter. I was not there when they worked with Modi in 2014, when people in CAG were working with RSS and BJP. I don't think their

---

[3] In late 2018, Kishor left the core IPAC leadership and now calls himself a 'mentor' to the firm. He is rumoured to consult as an independent advisor to a number of political campaigns, most recently for Mamata Banerjee in West Bengal. In 2018, he told reporters that he is 'done and dusted with being this freelance, in your words, ideology agnostic guy' (Express News Service 2018) who does the 'thankless job' of strategising for other political leaders when 'you don't have any control post a person's victory'. Although he later joined JDU, a regional political party in Bihar led by Nitish Kumar, he was asked to leave the party in early 2020 due to a disagreement over the Citizenship Amendment Act, which was passed in 2019.

way of interacting with them was very different from working with JDU in Bihar, Congress in Uttar Pradesh, and Shiv Sena in Maharashtra. I don't think the way we operate depends on the ideology of the party. What matters to us is whether we're giving a stable and good government or not. Whether the party we're supporting, if it eventually ends up winning, is stable and a better one than the existing one. That's how we usually think about which projects to get.

(Interview with current political consultant at IPAC, June 2019)

As this consultant notes, IPAC 'cannot be stringent about choosing the ideologies they work with', and tends to believe that political parties make opportunistic election promises based on what research shows their constituency will respond to. The way 'ideology' is referred to by this interviewee is not rigidly defined. Most of my interviewees are comfortable working for political parties' PR machines and debating the nuances of Hindutva without subscribing to any political party as an 'ideology'. Indeed, scholars of Indian politics have long debated whether 'ideology' as a coherent system of beliefs plays a role in Indian politics (Chhibber and Verma 2018; Corbridge and Harriss 2013; Jaffrelot 1993), many arguing that political power and defined party ideology in India do not necessarily coincide, particularly with the turn towards coalition politics in the 1990s. Among middle class, cosmopolitan Indians, 'ideology' is often used as a euphemism for identitarianism, criminality, and self-interest (Bhatia 2019). While this consultant notes that IPAC would like to work for a party that gives a 'stable and good' government, consulting firms primarily tend to work for parties that are able to pay them their high fees. If a party wins, they often have no role to play in their policymaking or decisions that might lead to what they perceive to be a 'stable and good' government post-election. Here, good governance is understood as a politically neutral sense of stability. Other consultants confessed to being drawn to the thrill of competition and the allure of winning, seeing political play as a sport.

While firms such as IPAC offer this politically neutral campaigning as a form of political participation, Kishor offers another initiative to make politics professional and clean. After joining active politics and relinquishing control of IPAC in late 2018, Prashant Kishor started an initiative called 'Youth in Politics' (YIP), attempting to bring young people into active electoral politics: the slogan reads, 'India is young but our politicians are old' (Kishor n.d.). This initiative sets up political consultants at IPAC as willing and able to provide mentorship to young, aspiring politicians. Young politicians are invited to learn from the 'political acumen' of Prashant Kishor and benefit from professional guidance and tailor-made mentorship plans from consultants at IPAC. As such, IPAC and Kishor have not only professionalised political campaigning but also are professionalising active politics itself. The former functions from a more explicit lack of political partisanship, and the latter offers itself as politically neutral while promising a platform to 'meaningfully contribute' to electoral politics.

The consulting fees charged by IPAC and other firms count on their consultants having graduated from elite technical universities. The introduction of anonymous electoral bonds into elections in 2018 allows political parties to amass large funds from business lobbies without any transparency about where these funds emerge from and which interests they support. This, then, primarily allows political parties that have large amounts of funding and/or corporate support to take advantage of this professionalisation. A former IPAC employee lays out the profile that matters to political consulting firms and to their clients: middle-class graduates from elite universities and/or branded pedigrees of work experience.

> Most of them did tech education, went to banks, and they got to know of this opportunity ... a lot of them are naturally inclined to try something new, and they're bright people. And Prashant [Kishor] doesn't care what background you're coming from as long as you're from a premier institute. And he lays a lot of stress on

that – IIT, IIM. He would categorically ask what college are you from, or if you're from a good institute abroad, or if you've worked with Bain, McKinsey. The background matters to him and we get management fees based on the profile the team has. You have to share it, and it's easier telling the politician that okay, this is the kind of profile that my team has, these are the sort of people I have working. It makes you more credible.

(Interview with former IPAC employee, July 2019)

The title of 'professional', here, lends them credibility because of their elite qualifications and lack of perceived partisanship, but also makes them easily transferable for hire by different political parties.

What They Do

Ideally, this form of strategic political intervention could do what consulting firms claim, which is to close the gap between citizens and their representative and increase responsiveness to citizens as consultants help candidates figure out what their constituents want. Yet few reports suggest that the research and strategising that go into the campaigns result in increased accountability or transparency. Instead, the use of data mining and analytics is being used to amplify two aspects of elections-as-showmanship: targeting and messaging. The distinction Kishor tries to draw in my brief conversation with him is useful: what is the line between *stifling* democracy (as he describes political consultants in the West) and *deepening* democracy (his hope for professionals participating in democracy in India)? An interview with the training-in-charge of the Congress Party revealed:

There was a time when the Congress Party, the Communist Party, whatever local politics was happening, involved large amounts of people in major conversations about the future of the country, or society ... they would involve a large amount of outreach in villages and personalised communications by what we call workers of parties. So in that context, ideas had to be fed and vetted in that extremely people-centric space. That has now become very professionalised. It's no longer a deeply personal kind of communication structure, and how much of it happens also is unclear ... Now, because polity itself has shrunk towards electioneering and brand management, it's a game show kind of space with very little depth and people connect.

(Interview with Sachin Rao, training-in-charge of the Congress Party, March 2019)

It would be idealistic to think that people-centric democratic practice was as widespread as Rao suggests before the intervention of political consultants and think tanks, and perhaps to assert as much would be, at best, overly optimistic. Nevertheless, such changes in the agents of election campaigning can arguably shift the practices of everyday politics (Sheingate 2016). Manish Jha, founder of Janadhar India, another political consulting firm, is quoted in a national newspaper saying: 'For us, our candidate is a product, voters are customers, and a constituency is a neighbour-referral market where local influencers play a key role, especially in rural areas. Our work involves identifying and managing these influencers' (Sharma 2018). Jha's statement is evocative: the political party is a client, the candidate is a product, voters are customers, and citizens are influencers.

In the 2019 national election campaign, economic issues were framed through nationalist rhetoric, such that people believed Modi's larger interest lay in what is good for 'the people' and for India's global glory. Despite record unemployment rates reported in 2019 and growing economic downturn, he claimed to understand their needs and ability to 'get things done'. The strong organisation of the BJP's cadre managed to transmit messages throughout towns, cities, and villages, building support on the backs of offered welfare schemes and strategic preference given to particular caste and religious groups in each region. Party workers and foot soldiers worked with two consulting firms, namely Jarvis Consulting, and Association of a Billion Minds

(Bansal 2019). Together, they reached out to constituents who have benefited from or been offered key welfare schemes from BJP and BJP-affiliated governments, and targeted messages according to the caste and religious demographics of an area. These targeted messages worked to further draw imagined enemies and encourage voters to vote for the party that would address the needs of their community. For example, a former member of the BJP disclosed how the party could appear aggressively pro-Hindu nationalist to some voters and development-oriented to others (Bansal 2019). They could sell themselves as anti-cow slaughter in Uttar Pradesh while appearing ambivalent to it in North-Eastern states where beef is more regularly consumed (Palshikar 2015).

Multiple interviews revealed how political consultants would do intensive focus group discussions in each constituency. They would station an informant in each constituency for several months leading up to the campaign, assign individual people to target each double-sided page of the electoral roll, and collect weekly reports. Simultaneously, they would prepare campaign jingles, posters, and slogans projecting the candidate as the answer to a multitude of different and sometimes contradictory desires. They accessed demographic data on caste and socioeconomic status available through land records, census lists, national surveys, electricity bills, and electoral rolls. This helped to target phone numbers through calls, WhatsApp messages, and WhatsApp groups, bringing together people of each caste, religion, and socioeconomic group. They would then collect data through call centre surveys, send recorded calls, and gauge interest by tracking how long people would listen to each message.

At the same time, the top leadership continued to reach out to party workers and supporters through a nationwide proprietary NaMo phone app, while social media and traditional media worked to circulate a range of desires appealing to material needs; aspirations of moral and material desires; and imagined enemies. A former consultant explained how this data would come from multiple sources and be supplemented by focus group discussions, call centres, recorded calls,

WhatsApp groups, and consultants assigned to each individual page of voter lists in a constituency:

> So you ascertain a certain fact from multiple places. We had a call centre where we would give different surveys at different points in time. It was concurrent all the time – where they would call people, ask a certain set of questions. We used to give IVR (Interactive Voice Response) calls. IVR is one sided information where you get a recorded call and it'll be like 'main Kejriwal bol raha hoon' [this is Kejriwal speaking]. So with that data we would find out, say if it's a farmer-specific IVR, we figure that the person who is listening to it till the end is probably a farmer. So we would track how many people answered their phones, how many people listened for how many minutes – we would have all that data. Then we'd ask them to give us feedback too, but this data would be passed on to our WhatsApp team, saying that these are the people who are interested, target them. They responded to the farmer campaign, here's the data, send the farmer information to them – saying this is our policy for farmers, if we come into government then we'll do x for farmers.
>
> (Interview with former political consultant, August 2019)

As a former employee of IPAC shared with me, the communications strategy of campaigns would evolve based on sudden spontaneous developments. When Prashant Kishor's IPAC was building a campaign for Nitish Kumar's regional party, JDU, in the 2015 Bihar state elections, Modi made a disparaging comment about a personality trait being in the DNA of Bihar. This, then, became a core feature of a Bihar campaign that was in opposition to Modi's BJP.

> You can't pre-conceive campaigns – you don't know where it will go once you start. So Modi went to a rally and made that DNA comment – and he had made a very personal comment on Nitish Kumar, saying there was something wrong in his DNA. Prashant picked that up, was watching that rally in front of us and was like, replay it, we'll form a campaign on that – that you have said Bihar has

something wrong in its DNA. So we ran a DNA campaign, it was a huge campaign, where people were giving their nails and hair and sending it to the Prime Minister's Office, and the BJP party office, saying you can do a DNA check where you can see if Bihar's DNA is intact. It was crazy – all of my colleagues were collecting nail samples.

(Interview with former political consultant, August 2019)

It is worth remembering that this election strategy targeting Modi was formulated by the same consultants that, prior to this, centred Modi as the bringer of progressive and necessary change in India's 2014 national election. This example highlights the consultants' spontaneous ability to creatively build resonant mass campaigns, yet also of their particular ideologically 'agnostic' positioning. While the technical skills they bring to their firms are mainly data analysis, perhaps more significantly what they bring is a world view shaped by an apolitical discourse of change. Indeed, this approach to civic participation incorporates an endless drive for novelty in campaigning and has the potential to dissolve more coherent structures of pluralistic politics. At the risk of simplifying and generalising across a vast range of approaches towards politics, a former IIT graduate elaborated on this approach to problem solving:

A lot of young people in India, a lot of engineers right now really revere Elon Musk and Steve Jobs – we really underestimate the impact these guys have. They've changed the world, built start-ups, and we've seen a big shift in entrepreneurial energy in India in the last 7–8 years. This energy not only translates into tech companies but also into politics. The idea of entrepreneurship, individual change. These things are coming from people working in tech who don't understand that way the tech world works and the way democratic society works is not the same. But they apply the framework of building Silicon Valley in Bangalore, so they think that they can change politics like that.

(Interview with tech commentator and alumnus of IIT, June 2019)

This positive change seems to be premised on a particular conception of moral good and civic participation, one determined more by entrepreneurial success with a by-product of 'public good'. Here, a conception of public good reflects Irani's (2019) 'entrepreneurial citizenship', a form of civic participation that can 'construct markets, produce value, and do nation building all at once' (2019, 2). What makes these graduates attractive hires to highly selective management and political consulting firms is twofold: first, the pedigree of an elite institution; second, the higher probability of their consent to privileging a techno-managerial approach to politics and policy that prioritises corporate deliverables without necessarily questioning their impact on democratic accountability and electoral procedure. Interviews with former management graduates revealed that they bring with them the ability to frame and solve problems within parameters that value particular client-service approaches. They do so through a seemingly unattached, almost ascetic approach to governance and politics. Innovation through the 'church of Elon' (as one IIM graduate called it), here, can generate progressive 'futures' not only for oneself but also for social change at large, in a way that has little to do with political representation, or the state (Irani 2019).

CONCLUSION

In a global age of majoritarianism, a shift in notions of legitimate expertise tends to flip received wisdom about populism as ousting established institutions. Instead, as this chapter demonstrates, technocratic experts can serve to strongly reify the ruling party's strategies of governance, regardless of who that party claims to represent. This post-ideological attitude towards participating *in* politics while staying *out* of politics has significant implications for democratic legitimacy. Indeed, political consultants are being hired to direct party workers, while democratic participatory voices are replaced by the influence of think tanks and consulting firms. While the political consultants and policy consultants this chapter describes may see themselves as being 'outside of' politics and governance – and thus outside of hegemony – their work of 'rational calculation' (Mitchell 2002) and, indeed, their perception of their work is at the frontlines of transforming everyday practices of governance and political discourse.

The increased hiring of consultants in governance to innovate and deliver creative solutions using their particular skill sets is, ultimately, borne from a loss of trust in existing structures of political procedure and policymaking. This emerges both from the perception of the breakdown of state capacity and overworked local bureaucrats, but also from the underlying belief that the state is unable to perform and deliver. Instead of working to reform state capacity and bureaucratic institutions, rebuilding forms of responding to citizens, and maintaining accountability, they see the state as continuing to deliver further centralisation and bureaucratisation through increased rules and regulations. Private policy and political consultants, then, see their mission as providing political parties and government bureaucrats with the strategic expertise to fix a defunct state and advance a more effective, efficient, and professionalised governance structure.

5   The Double-Sidedness of Hindutva

Inside the BJP's Think Tanks

Populist movements tend to use the constituent features of representative democracy to gain support. They challenge political and policy elites, channel public dissatisfaction with bureaucratic insularity, and promote a more direct relationship between people and their leader. In the Indian case, this has accompanied the discrediting of elite 'intellectuals' and attached a heightened credibility to acultural, apolitical technocratic expertise. As the last four chapters have explored, the influence of skyrocketing technocratic and political professionalisation over the last decade can be tracked through a growth in the participation of consulting firms, think tanks, political consultants, and the outsourcing of elections as brand management. The key here is that the government and political parties increasingly seek professional input from data consultants, policy professionals, and management consultants. This is not entirely new, but the extent of it has emphasised a shift in whose ideas are valued.

Against this backdrop, the BJP and its supporters have been building alternatives to what they call an 'entrenched' left-liberal hold over intellectual legitimacy. The BJP administration post-2014 has sought to legitimise and disseminate its ideas in distinctly different ways from the Congress regime between 2009 and 2014. During the Congress regime, the government's Planning Commission (created post-Independence as a centralised economic planning body) and the party's National Advisory Council included advisors from civil society groups, grassroots organisations, and NGOs who brought legitimacy and amplification to certain social activist causes (i.e. Right to Information, Right to Education, Right to Food) (Chacko 2018). While this participation may have done little to alter an overwhelmingly top-down structure of technocratic regulation, it still made space for dissent, protest, and critique. The BJP government has a vastly differ-ent relationship to ideas emerging from civil society and to external critique. It relies primarily on its networks spanning supporters, members, and affiliates of the Sangh Parivar (the RSS family). It tends to ignore, dismiss, or intentionally stamp out criticism from opposition, by building and reifying strong, resonant binaries of nationalist and anti-nationalist behaviour, and often uses state and civilian tools of violence and suppression.

The BJP has thus dismantled or co-opted pre-existing advisory committees, universities, and established research institutions. In addition, the BJP–RSS's relatively new think tanks present an alternative to these institutions, giving the party's political ideology and policy decisions a footprint in already established policy networks. In 2008, the BJP instituted its own 'ecosystem' of policymakers in two key think tanks (India Foundation and Vivekananda International Foundation), as a way to build elite support in the lead-up to the 2009 national election. The former vice president of the BJP called this a tactical shift: from being seen as just action-oriented to solidifying its own ideological underpinnings in a policy framework (Hebbar 2017). While the BJP lost the national elections in 2009, it won by a landslide in 2014, and these two think tanks provided personnel for many pos-itions within the central government. As Palshikar (2020) notes of the current Hindutva hegemony in governance, 'it shapes a consensus around what is to be debated and what is beyond debate' (Palshikar 2020). It attempts to draw boundaries around the norms of political and policy contestation. While it is important not to conflate the BJP's claims with their results, studying the presentation of these think tanks gives insight into how the contours of the intellectual elite, or, rather, who are considered to be the intellectual elite and/or 'experts', shift. In deconstructing their aims and the messages they put out, we see the binaries they enforce and the discursive techniques they use to frame a range of legitimate policy choices.

I have previously argued that think tanks represent a useful focal point through which to understand the interaction of populist and technocratic forces in Indian governance. This chapter delves deeper into two variants of the BJP's think tanks: actively political and actively apolitical. I pay close attention to the different 'vernaculars' of Hindutva. Due to the exclusivity of policymaking culture in New Delhi, and the relatively recent prominence of think tanks, their activities have remained understudied. I address this lack by examining the BJP's attempt to build centres of elite, traditional intellectuals of their own through think tanks, media outlets, policy conventions, and conferences by bringing together a variety of elite stakeholders in government and civil society.

Some scholars have characterised the BJP's think tanks as institutions of 'soft Hindutva' (Anderson 2015; Anderson and Longkumer 2018, 373), that is, organisations that avoid overt association with the BJP and Hindu-nationalist linkages but nevertheless pursue a diffuse Hindutva agenda. I build on these preliminary observations to examine internal conversations within the think tanks about their outward positioning, their articulation of their mission, and their outreach techniques. Through a study of the BJP's two most prominent think tanks, I show how the think tanks negotiate a fine balance between projecting a 'respectable' religious conservatism along with an aggressive Hindu majoritarianism. This chapter offers the double-sidedness of Hindutva as a framework for understanding the BJP's wide-ranging strategy, enveloped in new understandings of political legitimacy and ethno-nationalism in an era defined by secular liberalism.

I begin with a brief overview of what I am calling the double-sidedness of Hindutva: a force that is both self-righteously majoritarian and apolitically intercultural. In recognising this duality, I draw on other scholars (Anderson and Longkumer 2018; Reddy 2018) who have recently noted that new manifestations of Hindutva are adopting two similar movements, often simultaneously:

On one hand [we see] familiar assertions of ethnicist identitarian politics: sometimes reactive, abrasive, but always sharp critique of

the contradictions of liberalism and the many inconsistencies of
secularism ... On the other hand, paradoxically, are appeals to
neutralizing frameworks ... pride in indigenous, civilizational
heritage and inter-linkages between Indic groups.

(Reddy 2018, 490)

This chapter empirically and conceptually explores the manifestations of these double assertions. Indeed, the two think tanks
I examine in this chapter exemplify this duality. The Chanakya
Institute (CI) (a psuedonym) has denied direct links to the BJP or the
RSS, yet RSS ideologues have held and currently hold strong positions
within the organisation. Since the BJP gained power in 2014, several
members of the CI have secured powerful positions within the government: as National Security Advisor, Principal Secretaries to the
Prime Minister, and multiple appointments to the reconstituted
Planning Commission, the NITI Aayog. While CI claims to be independent and non-partisan, it self-professedly falls 'under a broad head
called nation-building' that institutions of higher learning and universities 'have neglected' (CI Mission Statement).

On the other hand, the India Foundation, a think tank run by
the General Secretary of the BJP, has relatively explicit ties to both the
RSS and the BJP. Rather than attempting to create academic, intellectual respect for Hindu civilisational heritage as CI does, India
Foundation's mandate is to explicitly 'groom' a new class of politicians and policymakers. I draw on ethnographic data collected during
a ten-week internship in 2017 and follow-up interviews conducted
before the national elections in 2019, to trace CI's negotiations with
furthering the BJP's hyper-nationalist politics through an objectivist,
academic legitimacy. Often, it pursues both an anti-establishment
and apolitical, civilisational call to national unity. I interweave this
with a discussion of how India Foundation, in stark contrast to CI,
follows its own politically interventionist mandate. As interviews
with their leadership demonstrate, IF's explicit desire is to occupy
the ranks of (colloquially understood) 'traditional intellectuals' while

also moulding a new class of nationalist policymakers. This falls alongside more rigid, yet cloaked, claims to Hindu nationhood. In the process, I show how both think tanks build an alternative sense of respectable intellectual legitimacy; consolidate Hindutva networks across political, administrative, and military fields; and build a 'mimetic' Hindutva intellectual culture.

THE DOUBLE-SIDEDNESS OF HINDUTVA

I offer the double-sidedness of neo-Hindutva as a core framework for recognising strategies that move through the political and apolitical. These seemingly contradictory discourses become Hindutva's strength. They allow it to function as a force that projects aggressive majoritarianism, while simultaneously claiming an anti-political 'neutral' face of civilisational purity and inter-religious inclusion. A large corpus of work details how Hindutva has entered the vernacular of various local political contexts, and is operationalised by political actors affiliated or not affiliated to the Sangh Parivar (Bénéï and Fuller 2001; Bhattacharjee 2016; Hansen 1999, 2018; Jaffrelot 1993; Reddy 2006, 2011b; Therwath 2012). A similar breadth of work exists on the language of rage and grievance (what Jaffrelot (2008) calls 'the art of being outraged') rooted in Hindutva's anti-politics. This anti-politics is, at its core, a critique of prevailing political paradigms that have governed post-Independence India: those of left-leaning, secular, universalist ideals that have enforced a 'desacralisation' of public life (Reddy 2006).

Typically, an anti-political movement asserts opposition to establishment political paradigms (Ferguson 1994; Hansen 2018; Humphrys 2018). I suggest that a variant of anti-politics is a claim to the apolitical, which sees itself as politically neutral, presenting the option of a social life that transcends or is separate from politics (what others see as culture that is 'emptied of religion' and politics (van der Veer 2007)). Scholars have, in recent years, tried to make sense of how (and whether) we can conceptualise ontological boundaries to the political, lest all of social life fall into this category and we regard all assertions of the 'non-political' as illusory. Candea (2011), for one, cautions against seeing those that claim 'non-politics' as only being farcical, deceptive, or enacting a form of overly determined politics. In our case, however, non-political claims (which I identify as similar to claims of being apolitical) of Hindutva do, more often than not, tend to coincide with its political organisations. Here, I refer not only to notions of generalised Hindu nationhood but also to other forms of anti-political asceticism that are more readily associated with social work, tradition, community, and other cultural norms that are 'clothed in humanitarianism' (Bhattacharjee 2016) and thus able to, ostensibly, abstain from active political matters. The RSS, for example, has always seen itself as a fundamentally cultural organisation focused on civil society and social work, yet it is also the core of the BJP's militarised, grassroots ranks.

In such cases, Hindutva's anti-political formations collide and give it more power. As Hansen (2008) and Reddy (2018) insightfully note, the contemporary anti-political offers itself as a rallying cry, providing both philosophical and affective liberation from the depths of ostensibly corrupt, dirty politics. Scholars like Wendy Brown (2015) and James Ferguson (1994) have argued that neoliberal formulations of governance have shifted the way human beings are governed, evacuating political struggle from certain situations in favour of an antipolitical technocratic managerialism (Postero and Elinoff 2019). Others have examined how Modi's call for 'development' has accompanied attempts to reformulate conceptions of the political. His rhetoric of development can, in this regard, be understood as an apolitical inclusion that seeks to transcend regional divisions towards a nationalised aspiration (Anderson and Jaffrelot 2018; Flåten 2017; Palshikar 2015; Reddy 2018).

This is a tension well represented by the case of the Ram Mandir movement. While the Ram Mandir has long been one of the BJP's key election promises, it has expanded into a matter of shared political aspiration and cultural nationhood. In this vein, Reddy's concept of Hindutva as 'praxis' explains that Hindutva has become a *mediating* political discourse, moving between ideological certainty and diffuse unrelated and negotiated formulations (Reddy 2011b). It is the language through which ideologues, critics, sympathisers, affiliates, and so on can strategically make their own claims.

While some notions of ideology understand it as a systematic and coherent body of ideas (Fairclough 2001), Hodge's (2012) concept of 'ideological complexes' suggests that contradiction is key to how ideology achieves its effects. Indeed, dominant and preferred cultural meanings tend to interact with negotiated and oppositional meanings in a continual struggle (Hall 2001). While Hindutva's many discursive threads might risk inconsistency, they still define the terms through which the sociopolitical world is discussed. This chapter argues that Hindutva's contradictions act as its strategic strength, yet at times I also suggest that they reveal tension, highlighting its fissures or fault lines.

My findings demonstrate that the BJP's think tanks attempt to legitimise its ideas and policies by building a base of both seemingly apolitical expertise and, what they call, 'politically interventionist' intellectuals. Contemporary Hindutva can be both explicitly political and anti-political at the same time: advocating for political interventionism (through the India Foundation), while seemingly eschewing politics and campaigning for an apolitical route towards cultural transformation (through the Chanakya Institute). However, contrary to critical scholarship that tends to subsume claims of apolitical motivation within forms of false consciousness or backdoor politics, I find that several younger researchers at the Chanakya Institute do genuinely see themselves as conducting politically neutral, academic research. Claims of being apolitical take the cultural and religious parts of Hindutva 'out of' politics, allowing it to be practised and consumed as a generalisable national ethos. Rather than wilful ignorance, their acknowledgement of the organisation's underlying ideology understands the heavy religious organisational undertones as more *cultural* than political.

The Hindu Right's aim is not simply to outrightly reject science or to claim conservative traditionalism, but to claim scholarly authority by combining 'the language of Hinduism [with] the epistemological imperatives of modernity and the nation-state' (Lal 1999, 163). They want to strip Hinduism of its myth and 'ahistoric sensibilities', and assign to it a 'purported scientific history'. In this vein, the BJP adopts several aspects of liberal intellectual culture, with its members and affiliates participating in or hosting literary and book festivals (Pondicherry Book Festival), cultural festivals (Festival of Indic Culture, Kumbh Mela), specialised or partisan TV channels (Times Now, Republic TV, NaMo TV), and educational conferences, amongst others. The 'mimetic' aspect, a term I use to indicate imitation of a pre-existing liberal intellectual culture, of this presence is both about normalisation and about gaining a larger respectability through institutions of modernity.

The BJP's think tanks not only try to legitimise the party's ideology and give their work intellectual authority; they also attempt to propagate particular paradigms of virtuous nationhood through both emotionally and cognitively resonant themes of collective belonging. In Gramsci's characterisation of political and economic struggle, intellectuals play a pivotal role in shifting discursive formations (Forgacs 2000; Gramsci 2000). In a liberal capitalist society, organic intellectuals tend to provide personnel for the coercive organs of political society, while traditional intellectuals are meant to create authoritative knowledge that leads civil society to consent to the state. Civil society and the state then co-constitute one another, forming what Gramsci calls the 'integral state' – that is, where civil society softens and integrates with the coercive elements of the state (Humphrys 2018). Any group that is struggling to gain political dominance must, then, 'conquer and assimilate "ideologically" the traditional intellectuals' (Hoare and Nowell-Smith 2005, 10).

To this end, the dissemination of information through educational practices has been shown to normalise certain frames of thought (Griffith 1979). Indeed, the BJP has sought to use schools, textbooks, films, music, and other cultural artefacts to legitimise, persuade, and propagate their party's ideals of nationhood. As such, a key part of the think tanks' mission is an educational one. The BJP's think tanks run a series of youth workshops, training programmes, and other short-term educational institutes to educate the youth with their 'message'. In an interview, former BJP MP Swapan Dasgupta pointed out that these fellowship programmes appeal to large groups of young people from all around the country. While many are already passionate about the politics of the BJP or the RSS, these programmes tend to recruit science and engineering graduates from elite institutions who are not as 'politicised' against the BJP (as social science and humanities graduates tend to be), and are able to apply their business-friendly skills to a political framework. Indeed, science and engineering graduates are highly valued by the current administration – their skills, technical ability, and potential innovation are encouraged and seen as relevant to technologically oriented economic growth (Irani 2019). These young people often see themselves as non-political or consciously support the aspirational, market-oriented rhetoric of the BJP while dismissing (or supporting) its communal narrative. In contrast, the Congress continues to signify an exclusionary, English-speaking elite to those who do not have access to the upper echelons of the establishment. These forms of public engagement elaborate on the think tank's main mission: to challenge universalism, which they understand to be the promotion of broad-based 'Western' ideas of culture, history, and civilisation.

INSIDE THE THINK TANKS: SPATIAL ORGANISATIONS AND CONSENSUS-BUILDING

Upstairs/Downstairs

A wooden oval table seats about thirty members of the Chanakya Institute (CI), a reputable think tank in the neat, green heart of New Delhi. Former military heads, diplomats, and senior administrative officers crowd the head of the table, while fifteen to twenty younger research staff sit further down. As they wait for the director, the mostly retired senior staff discuss Modi's visit to the United States earlier that week: 'Trump is a buffoon, he doesn't have basic comprehension skills.' Scattered chatter, cups of chai clink on the table. Moments later, the director walks to the head of the table, gestures to an empty chair next to his, and introduces a retired ambassador, a 'part of the family' according to the director. On the projector screen is a slide displaying the title 'Talk on critical importance of original research for think tanks with special reference to CI'. Applause. 'Indian think tanks don't do as much original research as Western ones do', the ambassador begins. What really is a think tank? It is 'a group of experts organised to study an issue and provide information, ideas, and solutions to problems posed by those issues', he says. He goes on to declare, 'A good think tank helps inform policy with work as rigorous as academia and as accessible as journalism. We are spared the sterility of academe and have the opportunity to influence policy'.

As younger research staff gaze intently at the ambassador, he continues: 'We belong to an institution that has to deal with the widest scope of possibility. We deal with the ethos of the nation, because there is no facet of national life that does not deal with national security. I know how much a think tank is influenced by ownership or funding, so we made sure that CI would not accept foreign or government funding. The Board of Trustees ensures that it should be independent and only accept funding from like-minded people.' At this point, there is vehement nodding by the senior members of the organisation around him. Some mutter their agreement, while one of the other founders chimes in, 'We are non-partisan, but we have been lucky enough to have a responsive government in power now'.

Following his cue, another founder of the organisation, a middle-aged former colonel, swiftly adds, 'Though we are not linked to the BJP or RSS, make no mistake, our ideology is distinctly right of centre. A strongly nationalist, India First, is the leitmotif of this organisation and we do nothing that undermines or damages the nation. This has governed this organisation'. There is nervous shifting around the room, exchanged glances by the younger researchers. While most think tanks tend to be somewhat partisan, this overt declaration has breached the 'neutral' academic sheen of their usual meetings. 'When we started, we decided we would develop in-house positions on issues and stick to these positions. Everyone should be aware of our ideology and our commitment. The cause is that our nation is bigger than the CI, and it is what we are serving.' Affirming nods around the table. Scattered note taking. The ambassador goes on to expound on the necessity of rigorous empirical and academic research so that CI doesn't simply become a tool through which to reiterate existing opinions, but can be 'path breaking' in its research.

This internal conversation perhaps exemplifies the primary tension within CI: of neutral academic objectivity and Hindu nationalism. While I began my work with them expecting to see this tension, I did not anticipate the organisation's ambivalent positioning to be its strength. Much like Hindutva overall, CI seems to derive its legibility and its credibility precisely from flitting between Hindu majoritarianism and neutral claims to inter-religious harmony. Indeed, maintaining its neutral, academic facade means that Hindutva is scarcely mentioned in conversations with and between higher-level research fellows. A younger researcher at CI told me eagerly that the organisation was filled with 'former military staff and right-wing sycophants, with an icing of Hindutva and an aroma of a think-tank'. When asked if the organisation is then considered credible, they responded vehemently, '[I]f any think tank has influence on policy right now, it's this one – it's full of heavyweights, former military chiefs, foreign secretaries, and so on'. Despite decrying the left-liberal university environment, CI's research fellows are visibly seeking to assimilate into the genre of 'legitimate' academic space. Yet there is a cyclical relationship between their research, analysis, and predetermined conclusions. Rather than acknowledging a compromised academic rigour, they are certain that empirical data will support their pre-decided 'in-house positions' supporting the BJP's politics. Their stance on foreign direct investment into crucial sectors (such as defence production), for example, has oscillated with the BJP's public position on this issue which, itself, has moved between support and opposition over the last decade.

Two kinds of research staff populate CI's ranks: individually eminent senior fellows and junior researchers. The top leadership and founders are former military leaders, diplomats, and retired or current members of the government administration. Senior fellows for research have varying affiliations to government ministries, alluded allegiance to the BJP or members of the BJP, while a handful have doctoral degrees in international relations from accredited universities. Although CI's ambivalence might lead to a lack of credibility within left-liberal intellectuals, its members have already-existing inroads to key decision-makers within the central government. It became apparent to me that the credibility of the organisation lies in the power and prestige of the individual senior researchers who are reshaping the composition of socially anointed 'experts' in the public domain. As such, it seeks to develop a legitimate voice through the embodied authority of its high-level research fellows.

The younger research staff primarily have master's degrees in international relations or region-specific foreign policy, and write the bulk of the research articles published on the website and in CI's pamphlets. A few researchers who received degrees at Jawaharlal Nehru University, a historically left-wing university, have to repeatedly deny suspicion of their 'anti-nationalism' (a term used to degrade left-liberals as the enemy) in internal staff meetings, and affirm that they are, indeed, nationalists. The senior staff decry the Internet and liberal media as presenting 'alternative facts' and assert that younger researchers should go to primary sources (as in ancient Sanskrit texts) for information as often as possible, rather than basing their articles on secondary knowledge and analysis. They frequently refer to the historical authenticity and genuine wisdom of ancient

Hindu texts, while criticising modern interpretations and English translations as neo-imperial. This negotiation exemplifies the intricate, delicate, and often breached dance between the boundaries of empirical research, religious texts, cultural mythology, and ideology, and the back-and-forth of creating new knowledge through referring to older, civilisational texts.

The spatial division of books in the library basement, and the architecture and decor of the building materially manifest this institutional disjunction. The basement houses the library – one filled with books on India's appeasement of Muslims, the RSS political vision, India's failed socialist past, and threats posed by Pakistan and China. Stocked magazines report a review of what Urdu press in the country are reporting, gathering intelligence and information about the enemy. Part of this is a wide set of bookshelves stacking green folders filled with news articles written about Pakistan since its inception in 1947. Hindu idols and scrolls adorn other walls of the basement. Upstairs, however, is where the administrative staff and researchers sit. Upon entering, one faces a large photograph of CI's senior leaders, Prime Minister Modi, and an assortment of religious leaders at a conference – exemplifying their claim to seek harmony in diversity. Here, form mirrors content: CI's project is to bring the ideological base(ment) of the BJP to the policy table in a way that rewrites and re-presents it to be in India's collective, national interest – a collective that it implicitly defines as Hindu. A deeply political basement library is filled with literature advocating Hindutva, decrying Islam and propagating stories of Muslim appeasement and 'Islamic imperialism', whereas the upstairs continues to insist on its non-partisan leanings and that the organisation has no religious or party affiliation. This double-sidedness is housed under the same roof, in the same building, with the architectural facade of a temple and statues of gods and goddesses within.

Other interns serve as sources of intimate knowledge in this space, as they are both part of this world and separate from it. They often secure internships because of family connections. Dhiraj, a young BJP supporter pursuing an undergraduate degree in economics in the United States, is the son of a former research fellow. He admits allegiance to the institution and the BJP while simultaneously critiquing it through facetious and self-deprecating remarks. On my first day, Dhiraj told me that the organisation is 'filled with right-wing nuts, but I'm of that ideological bent so it's okay'. Dhiraj's nuanced treatment of Hindutva as religion, apolitics, and movement is indicative of a new form of younger BJP sympathiser: savvy and cosmopolitan supporters who acknowledge the contradictions and dilemmas around Hindu-nationalist thought, and are able to position themselves in favour of and opposition to selective aspects of it. They are able to comfortably dismiss the 'fringe' elements of the *gau rakshaks* (cow protectors) as 'ruffians', but can support online trolling as necessary for the cause. He points me to several books that emphasize the importance of Hindutva ('except for when it goes too far'), talking about how it's necessary to reclaim unity and a defence against the forces of Islam and Christianity (from the West). Dhiraj disputes the narrative that 'Hinduism is a way of life' (as the Supreme Court stated in 1995), but maintains that 'we need Hindutva to maintain India's unity'. He is vocal about his awareness of the left-liberal debates on Hindutva, and uses it to signal what he sees as pragmatic support for his position. Such discourses of pragmatism are evident throughout conversations with senior technocrats and young savvy Indians who occupy these organisations, and are sometimes used to bolster a politics of grievance and temper expressions of rage.

While I conducted fieldwork in 2017, there were repeated, violent attacks around the nation against Muslims carrying, or being suspected of carrying, beef. These violent, mob-fuelled incidents were heightened during Eid, and, while they spurred several protests in the city against rising Hindu nationalism, internal meetings to discuss current affairs remained entirely silent about them. Instead, their conversations asserted that Muslims are the 'real threat' to a Hindu Indian social cohesion, and expressed outrage at the idea of 'saffron terrorism' (Hindutva followers who attacked Muslims and sites of Islamic worship), which many of the researchers believed to be a manufactured myth concocted by the mainstream media. There was silence about internal debates within the BJP and party politics, only a consensus supporting Modi and the current administration. The senior staff never discuss religion, because, to quote Dhiraj, 'it's a touchy subject'.

Building Missionary Zeal in CI and IF

Dressed in a crisp white kurta and pyjama, Manoj often sat in the library with several books scattered open around him: books on the RSS vision, appeasement of Muslims, and Christian threats to India's unity. He introduced me to an older scholar who wrote a book about the 2002 Gujarat pogrom, in which Hindu mobs targeted, murdered, and displaced thousands of Muslims in Gujarat. 'He has a lawsuit filed against him', Manoj tells me, because he 'proved that the attacks began with Muslims targeting the Hindus. They don't like to hear the truth'. He tells me doing a PhD is important, that being a professional researcher is 'a real career now'. He continues, 'A good career – but it requires a goal, a "missionary zeal"'. In the same breath, he asserts that while physical strength, arms, ammunition, and resources used to be the path of dominance in 'the time of hunters and gatherers', it is now about 'strength through ideas'. 'Not everyone', he says, 'is destined for everything – every police officer doesn't become exceptional'. No, he says. We must accept our strengths and stand with pride. He theorises his and the think tank's mission as requiring a 'missionary zeal', making a difference through the 'strength of ideas'.

The senior researchers could be said to occupy the position of Gramscian traditional intellectuals, those who see themselves connected to no particular social class and as autonomous and independent. The administrative head of the organisation, however, presents a breach of this facade, where he asserts Hindu his Hindu identity and declares a war of ideas that is being won through a 'missionary zeal'. As administrative head, Manoj perhaps exemplifies the Gramscian 'organic intellectual' of CI.[1] He is an active political organiser: no doubt a member of the RSS who disregards the farce of objective academia, but instead sees academia as a useful means through which to assert ideas.

The conception of 'zeal', in this case, is powered by a righteousness against a series of conflated others. The 'other' covers vast swathes of time: from British colonisers to Muslim invaders, to a post-Independence culture of secularism and left-leaning politics. In her study of Thatcherite think tanks in Britain, Radhika Desai (1994) too acknowledges the presence of 'zeal' as an affective category. As the most conspicuous psychological characteristic of religious sects on the margins, 'zeal' is a common attribute to think tanks founded on the intellectual margins: 'the intensity of belief, its unchanging character . . . the firm unwavering conviction, the abstraction and ahistoricity, the almost other-worldly belief that, despite counter-evidence, over the long run they will be proved right and a dogged attempt to maintain the purity of their belief' (Desai 1994, 40). An interview with a former director of CI reveals how this zeal gets written as an attempt to 'decolonise' knowledge:

> So what is it that distinguishes one think tank from another? There has to be a certain vision, a bit of ideology, or just an academic interest. You see, CI came up only 10 years ago and one need that was felt, that most think tanks in India did not have an Indian narrative. They had Western narratives, mostly, and Indian narratives coloured heavily by Western narratives. For instance, there was very little focus on what is Indianness, what is Indian culture. We're all ultimately cultural animals. All Indian thinking was heavily influenced by this intellectual thinking which was developed in the West, so it was felt that we needed to develop an Indian narrative, we must bring in Indian culture. We must have

---

[1] Much like Gramsci's organic intellectual serves a pedagogic role within ideological hegemony, Manoj frequently brought in people and 'studied' with them in the library, educating them in the tenets of RSS ideology.

confidence in ourselves, we must not be defensive when we talk about India, Indian culture, and so on. To develop an Indian narrative and to put Nation First – it was not a jingoism, but it is because, see what had happened was that over the years and centuries of colonisation, and all these attacks that happened, India's creativity more or less ended.

This emphasis on a decolonising imperative drives much of the Hindutva discourse of identity. This, in particular, calls to Partha Chatterjee's conception of the 'thematic' in anti-colonial movements which treats nationhood as an 'essentialist conception based on the distinction between "the East" and "the West"' (Chatterjee 1986, 38). In its current formation within elite organisations like CI, this notion paradoxically tends to replace one sociocultural elite ostensibly representing the West, with another upper-caste Hindu elite. The former director demonstrates a key aim of CI: to reframe an 'India First', implicitly Hindu narrative ideology as a righteous quest for self-determination. In many ways, this desire echoes the 'Indian renaissance' mission of Hindu nationalist–sponsored civil society events, such as the Pondicherry Lit Fest in 2018 and 2019. The inaugural theme of this literature festival claimed 'Bharat Shakti' (Indian Strength), following from Sri Aurobindo's declaration to 'turn new eyes on past culture, reawaken to its sense and import, and see it in relation to modern knowledge and ideas' so that 'out of this awakening vision and impulse the Indian renaissance may arise' (The Pondy Lit Fest n.d.). The 'Indian renaissance' thus combines both cultural and religious elements of Hindutva, yet attempts to separate it from its underlying politics.

While CI and other mimetic intellectual activities emphasise an anti-political, cultural renaissance, India Foundation goes further, calling itself the 'vanguard of politically interventionist think tanks'. Subhash Das,[2] the former head of IF, argues that political parties must develop clear policy ideas. He insists that Indians ended up as 'slaves'

---

[2] Pseudonym by request.

to Muslims and the British because they never valued their own set of civilisational political paradigms, and that think tanks like IF can revive a nationalist policy agenda. In our interview, he was open to discussing new ideas 'as long as they are nationalist', reifying a rigidly defined nationalism.

> *Toh yahan par koi bhi dikkat nahi hai. Agar aapka agenda hai yeh ki aap isliye aaye ho ki aap leftist ho, aur aapka agenda hai ki aap businessman ho, aur aapka agenda yeh hai … Aap bas ek cheez settle karo ki aap kya nationalist ho ya anti-nationalist. Yeh aap hi isko … woh bhi hum argue karne ko taiyaar hain. Par hamare agendas clear ho. Hum to ek aisi society the ki humne kabhi state ko value hi nahi kiya – ek hazaar saal tak. Tabhi toh we ended up being slaves for 1,000 years.*

[It's no problem if we have different agendas and different interests – whether you're a leftist, a businessman – all that matters is that you tell us whether you are a nationalist or an anti-nationalist. We're even ready to argue that! But our agendas need to be clear. Our problem is that our society has never valued our own state – that's why we ended up being slaves for 1,000 years [under the Muslims and then the British].]

Here, Das argues that all communities and groups have interests and ideologies ('agendas') that guide them, but that some of these agendas are more nationalist than others. If we allow anti-nationalist groups to gain political power, he claims, we ('true Indians') will effectively end up as slaves to them once again. This rhetoric establishes a form of nationalism that is at once rigid and loosely defined, but rests in the hands of a select few proven nationalists to determine. Das claims that the political class has abdicated its policymaking responsibility, and allowed so-called vested interests, identity politics, and interest groups to influence policy more than they should. With the new ecosystem of BJP's think tanks, he suggests that well-educated people without a political constituency (that is, a traditional political support base) can play a role in politically interventionist policymaking. India

Foundation sees the BJP's think tanks as a way for this upper-caste, elite, and nationalist talent to re-enter the policy-politics ecosystem:

> Policymaking has completely suffered in this country because those that are responsible for making policy have no accountability for it. They can write anything. ... Now we need to create a class inside the political sphere. In my opinion, we need to create a class within political parties who might optically be a minister, or a politician, but will ensure that the political agenda of the party is pushed. And they will now intervene in policy. And they will take over political policymaking. You're going to need people who will be able to help you deliver, with ideas, with energy, with capacities, with capabilities. So, that's why it's a good time, it's a good time for folks like us [without constituencies], otherwise, people like us had no chance in this country's role.

Das heads a think tank that works to build intellectual respect for the BJP's policies, yet sees this intellectual work as an active part of political organisation. He sees himself as intimately connected to his social class: a cosmopolitan, middle-class, upper-caste group without grassroots political constituencies, which can bring intellectual legitimacy to 'political policymaking'. At the same time, he sees 'folks like us' as young, managerial experts who can bring much needed order to interest-driven political play: thus, he brings both a political and techno-managerial rationalisation to his active Hindutva politics.

His metaphor of Indians being 'slaves' refers to a discourse of long-awaited glory for Hindus. It bleeds in, carries through, and affects the way that people relate to the state and to one another. The BJP has popularised a discourse of 'appeasement' by the former ruling party: claiming that the weak Congress government spent the last seventy years post-Independence 'appeasing' Muslims and minorities with handouts, affirmative action (known as reservations), and preferential treatment. This narrative has taken hold to build resentment, anger, and the Hindu sentiment of long-awaited glory. The claim of universal development then becomes code for the majority, positing universal inclusion while being deeply partisan. An interview with a prominent journalist exemplifies this shift from national pride to ethno-centric nationalist aggression:

> I think the Hindu self-perception has also changed. They were earlier seen as passive guys, who kept getting hit and didn't respond because they were passive or given to quietude. And now they have become very aggressive, and you know, from the time of, I think, Rajiv Gandhi's first slogan '*Mera Bharat Mahan*' [my great India], where Bharat suddenly became masculine. From there it's grown in stages, to today where it became '*Garv se kaho hum Hindu Hain*' [say with pride that we are Hindu]. Can Muslims say '*garv se kaho hum Muslim Hain*', you know? To now, where you say, 'whose country is it anyway? It is our country, who are you?' This is a civilizational war.
>
> *(Interview with a prominent national journalist,*[3] *April 2019)*

The aggression and desire to express a Hindu pride also translates to the realm of dominant forms of knowledge. As the head of another smaller BJP-affiliated think tank tells me of their work, '[Hindu-nationalist intellectuals] are a reaction to the intellectual suppression that took place from that arrogance that was visible for so many decades [from the left-liberal intellectual elite]'. He continues, however, by saying that this 'liberated' reaction needs to be rigorous, 'academic, measured, and intellectual'. He claims, 'We're not like the Marxists that say let's suppress thinking, it's only our line … unlike what they project us to be, we're not that'. There is a clear desire here to assimilate and occupy the ranks of traditional intellectuals, part of which is a projected desire for academic, measured debate. This otherwise anti-political critique of a Marxist-dominated political sphere, however, fails to acknowledge that the BJP

---

[3] Anonymous by request.

administration also relies on actively suppressing voices of dissent emerging from universities, activists, and even people's social media accounts.

OUTSIDE THE THINK TANK: OUTREACH AND EDUCATION

Both India Foundation and Chanakya Institute actively appeal to members of civil society through a range of public events. While CI relies more on mimetic appropriations, such as cultural festivals, book festivals, newspaper articles, television appearances, and lecture series, IF actively engages with the BJP's mobilisation efforts. By campaigning internationally for Modi in the 2014 national election, India Foundation played a critical role in organising financial and political support for Modi. As the most prosperous minority community in the United States, the average Indian American household earned approximately $100,000 in 2015, nearly double the US average (Pew Research Center 2017). In the 2014 and 2019 Indian elections, Hindu-nationalist Indian Americans played a significant role in campaigning for and providing electoral funds to the BJP. As their financial and political influence grows stronger, the diaspora's 'long distance nationalism' (Bhatt et al. 2010; Falcone 2012; Jaffrelot 2007; Therwath 2012) has had a major impact on Indian politics and policy. Organisations like 'Overseas Friends of BJP', 'NRIs for Modi', and others capture both the ethnocentric 'cultural' allegiance of the Indian diaspora, and their aspirational business-oriented visions of governance for the country. Such groups often facilitate the transfer of funds and financial support from the US-based Indian diaspora to the grassroots Hindu-nationalist groups in India.

Indeed, Modi's spectacular reception in Madison Square Garden in September 2014, merely four months after his initial victory, changed the core paradigm of how the Indian state interacts with its overseas nationals. In the early days of Indian Independence, overseas Indians were made to give up their citizenship and treated largely with indifference by the Indian state while facing racism in the United States (Bald et al. 2013). From the 1970s onwards, Hindu-nationalist groups in India began fundraising with the diaspora, appealing to their aligned interests as primarily upper-caste Hindus. The liberalisation of the Indian economy in 1991 led to an increased economic investment in non-citizen Indians, prompting the government to promise them multiple entry visas and commercial rights. However, Prime Minister Modi's aggressive campaigning to the Indian diaspora in recent years is unprecedented in the history of the Indian state. While his rule as the chief minister of Gujarat in the early 2000s led to securing business-based networks of support in the United States, as prime minister he has harnessed the diaspora as an instrument to project India's global strength. As Das explains, organising the diaspora became a key form of political interventionism led by India Foundation:

> The very fact that he went to White House through Madison Square, that he did Wembley, or that he ran trains in Australia ... this is a policy intervention. This is a policy intervention to give you an example where you try to change the way, so today you have a Minister who is thinking of how the Indian embassy can assist the Indian diaspora. Rather than treating them as third-class people who have escaped the country to which the Indian government owes no obligation, which was generally the norm ... So I think that's what is needed, that's the kind of work think tanks affiliated with you politically can do.

In September 2019, Modi held a widely publicised rally of more than 50,000 people in Houston, Texas, called 'Howdy, Modi'. In an unparalleled PR spectacle, President Trump attended the event and posed for cameras, hand-in-hand with Modi. The Indian Ambassador to the United States claimed the event was proof of the 'growing partnership between the world's oldest and largest democracies', and Indian Americans are the 'organic bridge' between the two. In India, Hindu majoritarianism has been justified through a narrative of historical religious persecution by Muslim rulers and British imperialists. Yet as the recent Citizenship Amendment Act (2019) in

India[4] shows, being considered 'authentically' Indian is increasingly determined by ethno-nationalist allegiance rather than rights to citizenship. As such, a non-resident Hindu diaspora has more legal claims to being Indian than millions of Muslim Indians who have lived in India for decades. In other words, the extending of citizenship privileges to diaspora Hindus and the marginalization of Muslim Indians has been accomplished through the same legislation.

Efforts towards transnational Hindutva are a significant portion of the BJP think tanks' intellectual efforts. Dhiraj at CI sang praises about the book *Being Different* by Rajiv Malhotra, a US-based Hindu-nationalist author, who has provided legitimacy to Hindutva intellectuals, including those at CI. Malhotra's 'breaking India' theory has gained popularity in legitimating the idea that Western forces asserting liberalism and universalism are attempting to disintegrate India's cultural and Hindu unity. Simultaneously, in order for it to appear cutting edge and contemporary, CI has cultivated a number of intellectuals in the United States, a group of historians based in Belgium (including the Indologist Koenraad Elst), and intellectuals within India who have affiliations with organisations in the United States and Europe. It is primarily this broad-based group of Hindutva intellectuals who are invited to give lectures at the institute. Senior fellows and researchers based in CI are also often published in English-language national newspapers (such as *Times of India*, *Indian Express*, and *Hindustan Times*), more niche right-wing platforms (the *Swarajya* magazine), as well as appearing in panel discussions on national TV channels, both private and public (Doordarshan, Times Now, Republic TV, to name a few). A few Hindutva publishing houses, such as Voice of India, publish academic works and claim to ideologically defend Hindu public culture.

---

[4] The CAA amended the Indian Citizenship Act of 1955 by providing a pathway to Indian citizenship for persecuted religious minorities from Afghanistan, Bangladesh, and Pakistan who are Hindus, Sikhs, Buddhists, Jains, Parsis, or Christians, and arrived in India before the end of December 2014. The law, however, does not grant such eligibility to Muslims from these Muslim-majority countries.

An interview with a research fellow at CI revealed their education-driven forms of outreach. Alluding to the organisation's larger lecture events, the interview emphasises the think tank's focus on outreach, education, raising awareness, and, crucially, an attempt to build nationalism and an attachment to the nation's symbols.

> [We host] one of the finest lecture series, and we do interdisciplinary work, get many people together from various disciplines and our halls are absolutely packed. And now we've also started reaching out to students and universities. For example last year we reached out to some 70 schools, and class tenth, eleventh, and twelfth. We wanted young kids to write about 'India of my Dreams'. And it was very good, some essays in Hindi and in English and many of them were Municipality schools, and we had a fantastic interaction – we selected five and interacted with their parents, teachers, students. ... We get the Chiefs of the Armed Forces, get some schools, get them to shake hands. See, the idea is we must generate good citizens, that's what's most important. Otherwise, we can talk to the converted, which is our standard work, but where there is a certain responsibility of think tanks also to the younger generations.

The focus he expresses is for the think tank to have a responsibility towards the youth to generate 'good' citizens. 'Good' citizens, here, refers to not only national pride but also a specific Hindu version of national pride. An interview with the same research fellow highlighted the particular kind of 'Indianness' that guides their thinking:

> When we look at a problem, we try to see it purely from the Indian viewpoint. We try to see, is this a Western narrative that I'm parroting, can I put something of Indianness here? Should I be impressed with a Western report, is there something in our past that relates to this? If you start asking these questions, then automatically Indianness comes. Then does it correspond to our

cultural diversity, our nation's objectives. Then also the kind of people you bring in. For example, we had a seminar here and we called it *Vasudhaiva Kutumbakam* [the world is one family]. Now nobody has done anything under this theme, and we did it interdisciplinarily – we tried to get Sanskrit scholars, historians, we had some people who are experts in scriptures, and tried to look at under this theme: can we build an Indian narrative that is useful for today's problems and issues of the contemporary world?

By trying to delineate a clear division between 'Western' and 'Indian' thinking, and implicitly tying Indian thinking to a history defined by Sanskrit religiosity, the think tank defines rigid boundaries of Indianness. Through their lecture series, educational outreach pro-grammes, and publications, CI attempts to not only reach high-level government officials but also to build an alternative intellectual space: through the public at large and, specifically, by targeting schools and educational institutions.

The India Foundation, in this vein, runs the Kautilya Fellows Programme: a ten-day workshop on public policy that primarily attracts science, engineering, and management graduates from regional and national universities. Prominent academics (including Swapan Dasgupta), ministers, and bureaucrats feature on the Academic Council, and the workshop involves a pilgrimage to the Kumbh Mela – the largest Hindu religious congregation in India. The Kautilya Fellows Programme runs in association with the Ministry of External Affairs, making clear the think tank's entanglement with the state and bringing Gramsci's idea of the 'integral state' to life.

There has long been a strong constituency within the Hindu middle classes who have found appeal in Hindutva rhetoric, even if public intellectual consensus in the past discouraged it (Palshikar 2020). Indeed, the recruitment of retired diplomats and administrative and military officers into the BJP's think tanks suggests that the Indian state system holds a reserve of officers with Hindutva leanings, either passive or active, who, after retirement, see their relationship with the think tanks as a continuation of their work while in service. What has changed in particular is the extent to which they are able to assert their opinions in the form of analysis (Tribe 1972). Several of CI's articles, for example, use considerable expository space to set up their narratives of oppositional politics, creating reductive analyses of how the 'mainstream media', 'sceptical commentators', leftists, Marxists, and a broad camp of critics approach the BJP, Hinduism, and Modi. Their articles begin by setting up their opposition's discourse and then moving to 'reason' a way out of it, glibly dismissing the magnitude or validity of this opposition and in many cases representing it as illogical, divisive, or gratuitously 'fashionable'. For example, in an article on the media's inability to fathom Modi, an author affiliated with the CI notes:

> One of the prime reasons for this is the deep-seated prejudice and even hatred for the Prime Minister, Mr. Narendra Modi and the BJP among commentators and the unwillingness to go beyond the moth-eaten script that sees everything through the prism of so-called secularism and Hindu communalism.... Therefore, it is fashionable to be Nehruvian or left-leaning. Those who do not conform to these two schools are to be treated as pariahs.

Many of their publications invariably have a section that dismisses left-liberal thought as a product of a colonised mind, primarily seeking to present a reductive narrative of it. In another published pamphlet called 'Policies and Perspectives', arguments against appointing Yogi Adityanath as chief minister of India's largest state due to his inflammatory anti-Muslim comments are forgiven as 'keeping with his firebrand image'. The author then appeals to the reader to understand that Adityanath is not opposed to any particular religious group, but any group that speaks and works against the country:

> Incidentally, he had sought to set the record straight during election campaigning itself, when he stated that he wasn't opposed to any

particular religious group, but to those who spoke and worked against the country. This cannot be held against him, surely.

The governing boards at CI and IF often occupy a rung between government positions and BJP–RSS leadership roles. As such, their primary success is not publishing reports but creating a venue that consolidates networks of elites across religious, political, and military groups. The research fellows affiliated to both the IF and CI have a fair amount of individual prestige based on their own political, administrative, or military background, and are able to disseminate the organisation's research widely through TV panel discussions, interviews, lectures, and newspaper articles. Through these channels, the CI disseminates hybridised discourses of Hindutva and national policy both implicitly and explicitly: through coding Hindu superiority as national interest, rewriting ethno-centric ideology as 'protecting India's unity', and defining Indianness and nationhood through a superior and ancient Hindu past. Indeed, the former director of CI expressed this desire to equate CI's mission as a path towards an 'Indianness' for all:

> You see, these ideas are for everyone. After all, everybody's an Indian, everybody's a citizen – this isn't about politics. It is very easy, after one or two conversations, iterations, we all talk along the same lines. Anyway, we don't have enough people who know about these things, we still have to build it.

In defining the organisation and himself as 'not about politics', he adopts an assumed objective neutrality. This pretension of neutrality feeds into developing a commonsensical understanding of what it means to be a moral Indian and nationalist: one that draws on a nationalism delimited by a Hindu, specifically Sanskrit and upper-caste, legacy. On the other hand, in perhaps the most explicit statement of the India Foundation's politically affiliated mandate, Ram Madhav actively speaks of using the think tank to build consensus for the BJP's ideological and political beliefs:

What the party thinks can be supported by the think tank by way of its own research, its own activities, its own conferences. For example, today the party and government think of One Nation, One Election.[5] Through the think tank we can do work, we produce papers on that, we do conferences on that. Things like that. Party policies, government policies, can be taken to an intellectual level, and presented to an intellectual audience, and in the process also benefit your speakers, your in-house intellectuals in the party.

Here, Ram Madhav acknowledges that part of India Foundation's key role is to produce research and organise conferences and external events that affirm the BJP's policy ideas in a broader, authoritative setting. They take the party and the government's policies to an 'intellectual level' and deliver it to a widespread policymaking and intellectual audience.

CONCLUSION

Part of the CI's and IF's projects have been to construct new markers of intellectual achievement. By claiming that higher education has been run down by left-wing politics and ideology, they attempt to build a counter-narrative to left-liberal intellectualism. They confess to being ideological only in their crusade for nation-building and national unity but, at the same time, believe this to be not necessarily ideology, but moral common sense. At the same time, they are caught in the double-sidedness of their mission: between the (claims of) politically neutral cultural facets of the organisation and its more overtly stated political partisanship.

As forms of 'soft Hindutva' (Anderson and Longkumer 2018, 373), the BJP-affiliated think tanks I have examined in this chapter try to foster two kinds of political and anti-political spaces: first, by actively 'grooming' future BJP politicians, and second, by producing

---

[5] One of the BJP's campaign slogans is to make one national election day rather than gradually rolling it out by state.

and educating portions of civil society to adopt a normalised, diffused form of a neo-Hindutva. Through CI, it is perhaps important to revisit Reddy's (2018) call to pay attention to the seemingly apolitical manifestations of Hindutva's anti-politics. While, in this case, CI does retain informal ties with the BJP–RSS network, many of the researchers within it see themselves as neutrally enacting formal academic research. This recognition ought not to be dismissed as mere rhetoric, as Hindutva crucially derives strength from constructing an imaginary that positions itself outside of the petty corruptions of Indian politics. This active experience of apolitical Hindutva is one of its most effective tools of resonance: it makes itself both visible and yet adapts itself into something banal.

Conclusion
Reading Indian Apolitics

During the COVID-19 pandemic, Modi and his supporters dissemin-ated pseudoscientific beliefs to assert the benefits of cow dung and cow urine in curing and preventing the coronavirus (Kinnvall and Singh 2022). In doing so, they reproduced a particular kind of far-right populism, fuelled through Hindutva pseudoscience that chal-lenged the tenets of 'Western' modern science and affirmed the hegemony of Hindu cultural fantasies.

People generally hold a cluster of beliefs, many of which are internally contradictory and not borne out in the social world. Indeed, we must not exaggerate the level of influence that intellectuals have had and can have on public consciousness. Yet in moments of polit-ical change or shifts in dominant perceptions of national identity, intellectuals and technocratic experts often try to re-establish the direct political relevance of their activity, reworking fundamental ideas about society. Their commitment, as cultural theorist Stuart Hall (1979) describes, is not only to reorganise elements but also to 'break the mould' – dismantling, reconstituting, and polarising the space to the right. The source of ideological belief, as in the case of Hindu nationalism, must lie in 'an already articulated and available alternative philosophy' that has a national historical grounded rele-vance and significance. Within these limits, intellectuals and techno-cratic experts have a strong hold on public credulity (Desai 1994, 38) and, particularly, legitimation in liberal democracies.

Successful hegemonic projects, then, require a passionate con-viction from intellectuals – not just Machiavellian strategy. Sometimes, this conviction is expressed as an anti-political oppos-ition to establishment politics and political play. The rallying cry of apolitical actors, for example, offers its audience potential liberation from the quagmire of political play. As I have examined in this book, this posturing likely adds to a normalisation, or 'banalisation' of Hindu politics (Hansen 2008). However, I also suggest that scholars resist the temptation to discount apolitical subjectivities and vocabularies as politics in disguise (Reddy 2018). By reifying the apolitical as only a form of overdetermined politics, we risk reinforcing rather than understanding the diverse logics that fuel Hindutva imaginaries.

The apolitical may certainly be, as critical scholars note, a failure to acknowledge power in social processes, but people do not necessarily experience their everyday lives as political, particularly when forms of Hindutva position their cultural and religious dimensions as outside of 'rational statecraft' (Hansen 2018, 229). While it might be challenging to see some of my interviewees as being 'outside' of politics as they claim, I suggest that such a world view exemplifies the sleight of hand through which actions and events are justified as either transcending the political realm, or working towards 'humanistic' goals. My empirical analysis in this book, then, has identified claims of being apolitical, technocratic, and neutral as layered and ambivalent expressions of pragmatism, agnosticism, and sometimes, political strategy.

Indian variants of anti-politics have offered, to the public, the possibility of 'separating the idea of the nation and its culture from the realm of instrumental statecraft' (Hansen 2018, 229). As an instantiation of anti-politics, the claim of being 'apolitical' gestures to a transcendence of the actively political space, what van der Veer (2007) sees as culture that is 'emptied of' religion and politics. In concluding this book about how multiple formations of technocratic neutrality and populist rhetoric combine to form their own unique political strategy, I suggest that the figure of the idealised antipolitical actor adopts a variety of the forms I have discussed: ranging from the (a) political ascetic and (b) the objective intellectual to (c) the proficient technical expert. The first kind, the political ascetic, can present itself through an asceticism that is more readily associated with social work, tradition, discipline, and other cultural norms that are 'clothed in humanitarianism' (Bhattacharjee 2016) and thus able to, ostensibly, abstain from active political matters. The RSS, for example, has presented itself as an organisation focusing on social work, yet it is also the training ground for the BJP's militarised, grass-roots ranks. The political ascetic can also be a 'brand', such as with Anna Hazare, a social activist who went on an indefinite hunger strike while spearheading the 2011 anti-corruption Lokpal protests.[1] As Hansen (2008) and Reddy (2018) note, the 'political ascetic who invariably disavows politics and calls himself a social worker' is the very epitome of anti-politics.

The second kind, the objective intellectual, can claim political neutrality by treating their work as a desire to expand realms of knowledge and a 'truth' underlying socio-economic processes. The Hindutva intellectual, similarly, projects an anti-political desire to separate ancient, civilisational knowledge production (i.e. 'pure' culture) from current 'dirty' politics (Hansen 2003).[2] Though anti-elite discourse criticises prevailing left-liberal intellectuals in the name of democratising knowledge, it has paradoxically led to further repression of marginalised Dalit and Adivasi intellectuals, while uplifting technical professionals, spiritual ascetics, and Hindutva intellectuals (Sagar 2019). For example, while engineering caste identities in order to win elections, the BJP has often furthered an invisiblising of casteist atrocities, claiming to have dismantled caste politics. In his 2019 national victory speech, Modi blamed people who 'play games in the name of caste', advocating for reframing categories within Indian society in economic terms. 'Only two castes will remain in

---

[1] For an analysis of the 2011 Lokpal movement and Anna Hazare as a political ascetic, see Hansen (2008).

[2] However, in much the same way that all claims of non-politics must not be seen as false consciousness, Van Dijk (2006) asserts that all knowledge is not necessarily ideology. While group knowledge based on a set of assumptions may be ideologically based, presupposed knowledge may be agreed on by groups across ideological differences. In addition, knowledge is relative to a community and often inter-subjectively 'objective' within that community.

this country. And the country is going to be focused on only these two castes.' He continued, 'The first caste in India is the poor. And the second caste is of people who contribute whatever little to free the country from poverty' (Sagar 2019). According to an *Indian Express* report (Verniers 2019), 'both the BJP and the Congress distributed nearly half of their tickets to upper castes candidates' – the BJP had 45 per cent candidates from upper-caste communities, while the Congress's upper-caste representation stood at 43.3 per cent.

The third type of the idealised anti-political highlights an instrumentalism at the core of the practical professional. As Irani (2019) notes, the 'entrepreneurial' citizen has become a key identity for a young, progressive, and aspirational professional: 'the entrepreneur as leader of the masses and agent of development' (Irani 2019, 39). This entrepreneurial citizen, however, is not limited to what development scholars identify as 'rendering technical', as in, depoliticising development interventions as only rational and instrumental (Ferguson 1994; Li 2007). Instead, the entrepreneurial citizenship model includes varied forms of epistemic, affective, and cultural diversity, promising them as 'potential resources for experiments in value' (Irani 2019, 212). A generalised glorification of the technically proficient expert in governance and politics has led to the outsourcing of both political campaigns and government bureaucracy to creative entrepreneurs in private management companies (Chapter 4). This 'new' technocratic managerialism has suffused a national imaginary of economic growth and technological advancement. Paradoxically, this technocratic advancement at times fuels and at other times contradicts the parallel populist surge of Hindu majoritarianism (Chapter 3).

Consensus-building legitimacy, as such, has to do not just with reason but also, of course, emotion – what *feels* right. We think something is right and good based on what 'feels' that way, appealing to normative ideas and sentiments behind rationales (to paraphrase one of my interviewees, in combining the prose of policy with the poetry of politics). Whether this book speaks to students or scholars of populist movements, technocratic managerialism, policy elites, or Indian politics, I hope that it contributes, in some way, to a growing corpus of knowledge on strategies of the powerful. Studying the politicisation of expertise provides invaluable understanding of how the right wing is able to construct effective narratives and be *convincing* of its multiple, potentially contradictory, formations.

The Indian government has waged a war on dissent, targeting activists, intellectuals, academics, students, lawyers, and journalists who question and challenge the government. This crackdown escalated during the national COVID-19 lockdown, using draconian sections of the Indian Penal Code and the Unlawful Activities Prevention Act to imprison dissenters. My emphasis on apolitical narratives of Hindutva highlights a key aspect of its cognitive and emotional resonance: that of both making it visible and adapting it into something banal. Through seemingly apolitical actors, political strategy is animated in struggles not only over power and status but also about morally and pragmatically superior ways to live. As I argue in Chapter 5, Hindutva's discursive contradictions are neither inherently good nor bad: they become a strength or a weakness in terms of how they are presented by key actors. As such, they leave potential spaces for their incoherence and contradiction to be realised as fundamental instabilities. To resist these overwhelming narratives, we must continue to develop knowledge and further research about how elite political and policy formations operate: who they work with, what policies they fight for and which ones they denigrate, and how they are materially and ideologically shaping the contours of our social worlds.

Works Cited

Abelson, Donald E., and Christine M. Carberry. 1997. 'Policy Experts in Presidential Campaigns: A Model of Think Tank Recruitment'. *Presidential Studies Quarterly* 27(4): 679.

Agrawal, S. P., and Rajeev Kumar Sharma. 1993. *Government and Politics in India: A Bibliographical Study of Contemporary Scenario Chronicling Rajiv Gandhi Era (Concepts in Communication Information)*. South Asia Books.

Ahmad, Aijaz. 2016. 'India: Liberal Democracy and the Extreme Right'. Idea of India, Background Papers, EMS Smrithi Series (June 2016). www.versobooks.com/blogs/3144-india-liberal-democracy-and-the-extreme-right (Accessed 11 July 2018).

Ajit, D., Han Donker, and Ravi Saxena. 2012. 'Corporate Boards in India: Blocked by Caste?' *Economic and Political Weekly* 47(32): 39–43.

Ambedkar, Babasaheb. 1941. *Thoughts on Pakistan*. Prabhat Prakashan.

Ambedkar, Babasaheb. 2014. *Dr. Babasaheb Ambedkar: Writings and Speeches*, vol. 10, ed. Vasant Moon. Ministry of Social Justice & Empowerment, Government of India.

Anderson, Edward. 2015. '"Neo-Hindutva": The Asia House MF Husain Campaign and the Mainstreaming of Hindu Nationalist Rhetoric in Britain'. *Contemporary Southeast Asia* 23(1): 45–66.

Anderson, Edward, and Christophe Jaffrelot. 2018. 'Hindu Nationalism and the "Saffronisation of the Public Sphere": An Interview with Christophe Jaffrelot'. *Contemporary Southeast Asia* 26(4): 468–482.

Anderson, Edward, and Arkotong Longkumer. 2018. '"Neo-Hindutva": Evolving Forms, Spaces, and Expressions of Hindu Nationalism'. *Contemporary Southeast Asia* 26(4): 371–377.

Andrews, Geoff. 2003. 'Technocrats or Intellectuals?' *Signs of the Times*. www.signsofthetimes.org.uk/pamphlet1/techno.html (Accessed 21 February 2022).

ANI. 2018. 'UP to Add "Ramji" as B R Ambedkar's Middle Name in Official Business'. www.business-standard.com/article/current-affairs/up-to-add-ramji-as-b-r-ambedkar-s-middle-name-in-official-business-118032900266_1.html (Accessed 7 May 2020).

Atherton, Gertrude. 1922. *The Bookman*, vol. 55. George H Doran Company.

Bald, Vivek, Miabi Chatterji, Sujani Reddy, and Manu Vimalassery. 2013. *The Sun Never Sets: South Asian Migrants in an Age of U.S. Power*. New York University Press.

Bansal, Samarth. 2019. 'How Modi, Shah Turned a Women's Rights NGO into a Secret Election Propaganda Machine'. *HuffPost India*. www.huffingtonpost.in/entry/how-modi-shah-turned-a-women-s-rights-ngo-into-a-secret-election-propaganda-machine_in_5ca5962ce4b05acba4dc1819 (Accessed 15 June 2019).

Banta, Benjamin. 2013. 'Analysing Discourse as a Causal Mechanism'. *European Journal of International Relations* 19(2): 379–402.

Barber, Benjamin. 1984. *Strong Democracy*. University of California Press.

Basu, Anustup. 2020. *Hindutva as Political Monotheism*. Duke University Press.

BBC News. 2019. 'What Happened in Kashmir and Why It Matters'. *BBC*. www.bbc.com/news/world-asia-india-49234708 (Accessed 8 July 2020).

Béland, Daniel. 2009. 'Ideas, Institutions, and Policy Change'. *Journal of European Public Policy* 16(5): 701–718.

Bénéï, Véronique, and Chris J. Fuller. 2001. 'Teaching Nationalism in Maharashtra Schools'. In *The Everyday State and Society in Modern India*, eds. Véronique Bénéï and Chris J. Fuller. Hurst & Co., pp. 194–220.

Berezin, Mabel. 2009. *Illiberal Politics in Neoliberal Times*. Cambridge University Press.

Betta, Michela. 2016. *Ethicmentality – Ethics in Capitalist Economy, Business, and Society*. Springer.

Bharatiya Janata Party. 2004. 'Discussion Paper on Tasks Ahead: Immediate and Long-Term'. *Meeting of the National Executive*. http://library.bjp.org/jspui/bitstream/123456789/251/2/Policy%20Document.pdf (Accessed 20 August 2020).

Bharti, Nitin Kumar. 2018. 'Wealth Inequality, Class and Caste in India, 1961–2012'. *World Inequality Lab, Paris School of Economics*. https://wid.world/document/n-k-bharti-wealth-inequality-class-and-caste-in-india-1961-2012/ (Accessed 20 August 2020).

Bhatia, Avnish K. 2019. *How Rationale Is Indian Politics?* Prowess Publishing.

Bhatt, Amy, Madhavi Murty, and Priti Ramamurthy. 2010. 'Hegemonic Developments: The New Indian Middle Class, Gendered Subalterns, and Diasporic Returnees in the Event of Neoliberalism'. *Signs* 36(1): 127–152.

Bhatt, Chetan. 2001. *Hindu Nationalism: Origins, Ideologies and Modern Myths*. Routledge.

Bhattacharjee, Malini. 2016. 'Seva, Hindutva, and the Politics of Post-Earthquake Relief and Reconstruction in Rural Kutch'. *Asian Ethnology* 75(1): 75–104.

Bickerton, Christopher J., and Carlo Invernizzi Accetti. 2017. 'Populism and Technocracy'. In *The Oxford Handbook of Populism*, eds. Cristóbal Rovira Kaltwasser et al. Oxford University Press.

Bickerton, Christopher J., and Carlo Invernizzi Accetti. 2021. 'The Concept of Technopopulism'. In *Technopopulism*. Oxford University Press, pp. 17–38.

Blackwell, Christopher W. 2003. 'The Development of Athenian Democracy'. In *Athenian Law in Its Democratic Context*, ed. Adriaan Lanni (Center for Hellenic Studies On-Line Discussion Series). The Stoa Consortium.

Bonikowski, Bart. 2017. 'Ethno-Nationalist Populism and the Mobilization of Collective Resentment'. *The British Journal of Sociology* 68 Suppl. 1: S181–S213.

Brown, Wendy. 2015. *Undoing the Demos: Neoliberalism's Stealth Revolution*. MIT Press.

Bruff, Ian. 2014. 'The Rise of Authoritarian Neoliberalism'. *Rethinking Marxism* 26 (1): 113–129.

Buštíková, Lenka. 2019. *Extreme Reactions*. Cambridge University Press.

Cain, Sean A. 2011. 'An Elite Theory of Political Consulting and Its Implications for U.S. House Election Competition'. *Political Behavior* 33(3): 375–405.

Candea, Matei. 2011. 'Making a Space for the Non-political in the Anthropology of Politics'. *Current Anthropology* 52(3): 309–334.

Caramani, Daniele. 2017. 'Will vs. Reason: The Populist and Technocratic Forms of Political Representation and Their Critique to Party Government'. *Political Analysis: An Annual Publication of the Methodology Section of the American Political Science Association* 111(1): 54–67.

Centeno, Miguel Angel. 2010. *Democracy within Reason: Technocratic Revolution in Mexico*. Penn State Press.

Chacko, Priya. 2018. 'The Right Turn in India: Authoritarianism, Populism and Neoliberalisation'. *Journal of Contemporary Asia* 48(4): 541–565.

Chacko, Priya. 2019. 'Marketizing Hindutva: The State, Society, and Markets in Hindu Nationalism'. *Modern Asian Studies* 53(2): 377–410.

Chakravartty, Paula. 2004. 'Telecom, National Development and the Indian State: a Postcolonial Critique'. *Media Culture & Society* 26(2): 227–249.

Chatterjee, Partha. 1986. *Nationalist Thought and the Colonial World: A Derivative Discourse?* Zed Books.

Chatterjee, Partha. 1993. *The Nation and Its Fragments: Colonial and Postcolonial Histories*. Princeton University Press.

Chatterjee, Partha. 2008. 'Democracy and Economic Transformation in India'. *Economic and Political Weekly* 43(16): 53–62.

Chatterjee, Partha. 2011. *Lineages of Political Society: Studies in Postcolonial Democracy*. Columbia University Press.

Chaturvedi, Swati. 2016. *I Am a Troll: Inside the Secret World of the BJP's Digital Army*. Juggernaut Books.

Chauchard, Simon. 2018. 'Electoral Handouts in Mumbai Elections'. *Asian Survey* 58(2): 341–364.

Chhibber, Pradeep K., and Rahul Verma. 2014. 'The BJP's 2014 "Modi Wave": An Ideological Consolidation of the Right'. *Economic and Political Weekly* 49 (39): 50–56.

Chhibber, Pradeep K., and Rahul Verma. 2018. *Ideology and Identity: The Changing Party Systems of India*. Reprint edition. Oxford University Press.

Choudhury, Savitri, and Suveen Sinha. 2004. 'The Firm's Follies'. *Outlook Magazine*. www.outlookindia.com/magazine/story/the-firms-follies/225371 (Accessed 20 November 2019).

Clarke, John, and Janet Newman. 1997. *The Managerial State: Power, Politics and Ideology in the Remaking of Social Welfare*. Sage.

Corbridge, Stuart, and John Harriss. 2013. *Reinventing India: Liberalization, Hindu Nationalism and Popular Democracy*. John Wiley & Sons.

Cox, Michael, and E. H. Carr. 2001. *244 The Twenty Years' Crisis, 1919–1939: An Introduction to the Study of International Relations*, eds. Michael Cox and E. H. Carr. Palgrave Macmillan.

Das, Upasak, and Diego Maiorano. 2019. 'Post-clientelistic Initiatives in a Patronage Democracy: The Distributive Politics of India's MGNREGA'. *World Development* 117: 239–252.

Dasgupta, Swapan. 2018. 'Cry Fascism! Modi Critics Fall Back on Oldest Trick in Politics'. *Times of India*. https://timesofindia.indiatimes.com/blogs/right-and-wrong/cry-fascism-modi-critics-fall-back-on-oldest-trick-in-politics/ (Accessed 22 February 2022).

Davies, Bronwyn. 2003. 'Death to Critique and Dissent? The Policies and Practices of New Managerialism and of "Evidence-Based Practice"'. *Gender and Education* 15(1): 91–103.

Desai, Radhika. 1994. 'Second-Hand Dealers in Ideas: Think-Tanks and Thatcherite Hegemony'. *New Left Review* 27–27.

Desai, Radhika. 2014. 'A Latter Day Fascism'. *Economic and Political Weekly* 49 (35): 48–58.

Desai, Radhika. 2016. 'Neo-Liberalism and Cultural Nationalism: A Danse Macabre'. In *Neoliberal Hegemony: A Global Critique*, eds. Dieter Plehwe et al. Routledge.

Desai, Santosh. 2019. 'New Elite vs Liberals: The Rift Widens'. *Times of India Blog*. https://timesofindia.indiatimes.com/blogs/Citycitybangbang/new-elite-vs-liberals-the-rift-widens/ (Accessed 19 July 2020).

Desai, Vandana, and Rob Imrie. 1998. 'The New Managerialism in Local Governance: North-South Dimensions'. *Third World Quarterly* 19(4): 635–650.

Dhattiwala, Raheel, and Michael Biggs. 2012. 'The Political Logic of Ethnic Violence: The Anti-Muslim Pogrom in Gujarat, 2002'. *Politics & Society* 40 (4): 483–516.

Dhingra, Sanya. 2018. 'Hard Fact: Despite Quotas, Dalits, Tribals Are Nowhere in Delhi's Corridors of Power'. *ThePrint*. https://theprint.in/opinion/dalit-history-month/despite-quotas-dalits-tribals-are-nowhere-in-delhis-corridors-of-power/50167/ (Accessed 23 July 2020).

Digital Desk. 2021. 'Ayodhya Ram Temple to Be a Marvel of Modern Technology and Ancient Heritage'. *Republic World*. www.republicworld.com/india-news/general-news/ayodhya-ram-temple-to-be-a-marvel-of-modern-technology-and-ancient-heritage.html (Accessed 22 February 2023).

Dillow, Chris. 2007. *The End of Politics: New Labour and the Folly of Managerialism*. Harriman House.

Domhoff, G. William. 2010. *Who Rules America? Challenges to Corporate and Class Dominance*. McGraw Hill Higher Education.

Dutta, Anisha. 2019. 'How BJP Used Data to Craft Landslide Win'. *Hindustan Times*. www.hindustantimes.com/lok-sabha-elections/how-bjp-used-data-to-craft-landslide-win/story-A3dNXdPiaG9pTVMf6j8mEJ.html (Accessed 12 June 2020).

Elliott, Carolyn. 2011. 'Moving from Clientelist Politics toward a Welfare Regime: Evidence from the 2009 Assembly Election in Andhra Pradesh'. *Commonwealth & Comparative Politics* 49(1): 48–79.

Elyachar, Julia. 2012. 'Next Practices: Knowledge, Infrastructure, and Public Goods at the Bottom of the Pyramid'. *Public Culture* 24(1 (66)): 109–129.

Equal Rights for Hindus. 'Hindu Charter of Demands'. *Equal Rights for Hindus*. www.equalrightsforhindus.com/ (Accessed 21 February 2022).

Etzioni-Halevy, Eva. 2013. *Bureaucracy and Democracy*. Routledge.

Express News Service. 2018. '"Modi is a big leader, but generating 2014-style hype again is hard", Says JD(U) Vice-President Prashant Kishor'. *The Indian Express*. https://indianexpress.com/article/india/pm-modi-is-a-big-leader-2014-style-hype-jdu-vice-president-prashant-kishor-bjp-2019-lok-sabha-polls-5440731/ (Accessed 23 February 2022).

Fairclough, Norman. 2001. *Language and Power, 1989*. Longman.

Falcone, Jessica Marie. 2012. 'Putting the "Fun" in Fundamentalism: Religious Nationalism and the Split Self at Hindutva Summer Camps in the United States'. *Ethos* 40(2): 164–195.

Ferguson, James. 1994. *The Anti-politics Machine: "Development," Depoliticization, and Bureaucratic Power in Lesotho*. University of Minnesota Press.

Financial Express. 2020. 'Ayodhya Ram Mandir Bhumi Pujan Photos: Wearing Traditional Dhoti-Kurta, PM Modi Performs "bhumi pujan"'. *The Financial Express*. https://www.financialexpress.com/photos/lifestyle-gallery/2127882/ayodhya-deepotsav-2020-stunning-images-festival-lamps-diyas-guinness-world-record-ram-janmabhoomi-up-yogi-adityanath/ (Accessed 10 August 2020).

Firstpost. 2016. 'Narendra Modi in Goa Full Text: Once We Get Clean, We Need Not Worry About Even One Corrupt Mosquito – Firstpost'. *Firstpost.* www.firstpost .com/politics/narendra-modi-in-goa-full-text-once-we-get-clean-we-need-not-worry-about-even-one-corrupt-mosquito-3103608.html (Accessed 17 January 2020).

Firstpost. 2019. 'Ayodhya Verdict: SC Hands Entire Disputed Structure to Hindus but Holds Babri Demolition Was Illegal; Key Highlights from Judgment'. *Firstpost.* www .firstpost.com/india/ayodhya-verdict-sc-hands-entire-disputed-structure-to-hindus-but-holds-babri-demolition-was-illegal-key-highlights-from-judgment-7626191.html (Accessed November 2020).

Firstpost. 2020. 'Ayodhya Ram Mandir bhumi pujan: Narendra Modi Likens Fight for Temple to Freedom Struggle, Says Ram Belongs to All'. *Firstpost.* www.firstpost.com/ india/ayodhya-ram-mandir-bhumi-pujan-narendra-modi-likens-fight-for-temple-to-freedom-struggle-says-ram-belongs-to-all-8675061.html (Accessed 10 August 2020).

Fischer, Frank. 2002. 'Policy Discourse and the Politics of Washington Think Tanks'. In *The Argumentative Turn in Policy Analysis and Planning,* eds. Frank Fischer and John Forester. Routledge, pp. 29–50.

Fischer, Frank. 2004. 'Professional Expertise in a Deliberative Democracy'. *The Good Society* 13(1): 21–27.

Fischer, Frank, Douglas Torgerson, Anna Durnová, and Michael Orsini. 2015. *Handbook of Critical Policy Studies.* Edward Elgar.

Flåten, Lars Tore. 2017. 'Spreading Hindutva through Education: Still a Priority for the BJP?' *India Review* 16(4): 377–400. http://dx.doi.org/10.1080/14736489 .2017.1378481.

Forgacs, David, ed. 2000. *The Gramsci Reader.* NYU Press.

Foucault, Michel. 2012. *The Archaeology of Knowledge.* Knopf Doubleday.

Foucault, Michel, Arnold I. Davidson, and Graham Burchell. 2008. *The Birth of Biopolitics: Lectures at the Collège de France, 1978–1979.* Springer.

Ghassem-Fachandi, Parvis. 2012. *Hindu Nationalism and Anti-Muslim Violence in India.* Princeton University Press.

Golwalkar, M. S. 1939. *We, or Our Nationhood Defined.* Bharat Publications.

Golwalkar, M. S. 1966. *A Bunch of Thoughts.* Vikram Prakashan.

Gramsci, Antonio. 2000. *The Gramsci Reader: Selected Writings, 1916–1935.* NYU Press.

Grey, Christopher. 1999. '"We are all managers now"; "we always were": On the Development and Demise of Management'. *Journal of Management Studies* 36 (5): 561–585.

Griffith, William E. 1979. 'Communist Propaganda'. *Propaganda and Communication in World History* 2: 234–241.

Gudavarthy, Ajay. 2018. 'How BJP Appropriated the Idea of Equality to Create a Divided India'. *Economic and Political Weekly* 53(17). www.epw.in/node/ 151662/pdf.

Guha, Ramachandra. 2015. 'Ramachandra Guha Contemplates the Lack of Right-Wing Intellectuals in Three Key Disciplines'. *The Caravan*. https://caravanmagazine.in/vantage/ramachandra-guha-right-wing-intellectuals-history-political-science-economics (Accessed 15 July 2020).

Gupta, Akhil. 1995. 'Blurred Boundaries: The Discourse of Corruption, the Culture of Politics, and the Imagined State'. *American Ethnologist* 22(2): 375–402.

Gupta, Akhil. 2012. *Red Tape: Bureaucracy, Structural Violence, and Poverty in India*. Duke University Press.

Gupta, Rajendra Pratap. 2019. 'BJP Manifesto: Lateral Entry, a Radical Reform but Not Enough to Change System'. *The Economic Times*. https://economictimes.indiatimes.com/news/politics-and-nation/view-lateral-entry-a-radical-reform-but-not-enough-to-change-system/articleshow/68983462.cms?from=mdr (Accessed 12 November 2019).

Guru, Gopal, and Sundar Sarukkai. 2018. *The Cracked Mirror: An Indian Debate on Experience and Theory*. Oxford University Press.

Haas, Peter M. 1992. 'Introduction: Epistemic Communities and International Policy Coordination'. *International Organization* 46(1): 1–35.

Haidar, Suhasini. 2019. 'RSS Is a Mass Movement, Part of Indian "Mosaic": German Envoy Walter Lindner'. *The Hindu*. www.thehindu.com/news/national/rss-is-a-mass-movement-part-of-indian-mosaic-german-envoy/article61593247.ece (Accessed 26 February 2022).

Hall, Stuart. 1979. 'The Great Moving Right Show'. *Marxism Today* 23(1): 14–20.

Hall, Stuart. 1985. 'Authoritarian Populism: A Reply'. *New Left Review* (151): 115. https://newleftreview.org/issues/i151/articles/stuart-hall-authoritarian-populism-a-reply (Accessed September 2020).

Hall, Stuart. 2001. 'Encoding/Decoding'. *Media and Cultural Studies: Keyworks* 16676. https://books.google.com/books?hl=en&lr=&id=I8dPhB88Sx4C&oi=fnd&pg=PA163&dq=hall+encoding/decoding&ots=CE_yrHaFhM&sig=g7vJWcbXRvnBavL6TqwvBK4JbWw.

Hallas, Duncan. 1983. 'Duncan Hallas: Marx, Engels and the Vote (June 1983)'. www.marxists.org/archive/hallas/works/1983/06/vote.htm (Accessed 4 November 2019).

Hansen, Thomas Blom. 1999. *The Saffron Wave: Democracy and Hindu Nationalism in Modern India*. Princeton University Press.

Hansen, Thomas Blom. 2003. 'Predicaments of Secularism: Muslim Identities and Politics in Mumbai'. *The Journal of the Royal Anthropological Institute* 6(2): 255–272.

Hansen, Thomas Blom. 2008. 'The Political Theology of Violence in Contemporary India'. *South Asia Multidisciplinary Academic Journal* (2). https://journals.openedition.org/samaj/1872.

Hansen, Thomas Blom. 2018. *Wages of Violence: Naming and Identity in Postcolonial Bombay*. Princeton University Press.

Hansen, Thomas Blom, and Christophe Jaffrelot, eds. 1998. *The BJP and the Compulsions of Politics in India*. Oxford University Press.

Hasan, Nafis A. 2021. 'Techno-Politics of Information and Communication Technologies (ICTs): Investigating Material Practices and Social Relations in Indian Public Bureaucracies'. *UCLA*. https://escholarship.org/uc/item/0k7826v9 (Accessed 23 February 2022).

Havelka, Milos. 2016. '"Anti-politics", "Non-political Politics" and "Sub-politics" as Threats and Challenges'. *Sociální Studia / Social Studies* 13(1): 9–22.

Hebbar, Nistula. 2017. 'At Mid-Term, Modi's BJP on Cusp of Change'. *The Hindu*. www.thehindu.com/thread/politics-and-policy/at-mid-term-modis-bjp-on-cusp-of-change/article18966137.ece (Accessed 15 January 2020).

Helleiner, Eric. 2021. 'The Return of National Self-Sufficiency? Excavating Autarkic Thought in a De-Globalizing Era'. *International Studies Review* 23 (3): 933–957.

Herzfeld, Michael. 1993. *The Social Production of Indifference*. University of Chicago Press.

Hilgers, Mathieu, and Eric Mangez. 2014. *Bourdieu's Theory of Social Fields: Concepts and Applications*. Routledge.

Hoare, Quintin, and Geoffrey Nowell-Smith. 2005. *Selections from Prison Notebooks*. Lawrence & Wishart.

Hodge, Bob. 2012. 'Ideology, Identity, Interaction: Contradictions and Challenges for Critical Discourse Analysis'. *Critical Approaches to Discourse Analysis across Disciplines* 5(2): 1–18.

Hofstadter, Richard. 2012. *Anti-Intellectualism in American Life*. Knopf Doubleday Publishing Group.

Honig, Dan, and Lant Pritchett. 2019. 'The Limits of Accounting-Based Accountability in Education (and far beyond): Why More Accounting Will Rarely Solve Accountability Problems 1'. https://riseprogramme.org/sites/default/files/2020-11/RISE_WP-030_Honig_Pritchett.pdf (Accessed 23 January 2022).

Howarth, David. 2010. 'Power, Discourse, and Policy: Articulating a Hegemony Approach to Critical Policy Studies'. *Critical Policy Studies* 3(3–4): 309–335.

Humphrys, Elizabeth. 2018. 'Anti-Politics, the Early Marx and Gramsci's "Integral State"'. *Thesis Eleven* 147(1): 29–44.

India Today. 2015. 'Modi Accuses Congress of Renaming Vajpayee's Schemes'. *India Today*. www.indiatoday.in/india/north/story/narendra-modi-bjp-congress-vajpayee-parliament-rajya-sabha-242857-2015-03-03 (Accessed 9 February 2022).

Indian Express. 2020. 'Congress Breaks Silence on Ayodhya Event, Priyanka Gandhi Says Lord Ram Belongs to Everybody'. *The Indian Express*. https://

indianexpress.com/article/india/priyanka-gandhi-hopes-groundbreaking-cere
mony-of-ram-temple-becomes-marker-of-national-unity-6538640/   (Accessed
11 August 2020).

Irani, Lilly. 2019. *Chasing Innovation: Making Entrepreneurial Citizens in Modern
India*. Princeton University Press.

ISPP. 2019. 'Indian School of Public Policy'. *ISPP*. www.ispp.org.in/ (Accessed
23 February 2022).

Iyengar, Shanto, Gaurav Sood, and Yphtach Lelkes. 2012. 'Affect, Not Ideology:
A Social Identity Perspective on Polarization'. *Public Opinion Quarterly* 76(3):
405–431.

Jackson, Richard, Eamon Murphy, and Scott Poynting, eds. 2011. *Contemporary
State Terrorism: Theory and Practice*. Routledge.

Jaffrelot, Christophe. 1993. 'Hindu Nationalism: Strategic Syncretism in Ideology
Building'. *Economic and Political Weekly* 28(12/13): 517–524.

Jaffrelot, Christophe. 2003. *India's Silent Revolution: The Rise of the Lower Castes
in North India*. Orient Blackswan.

Jaffrelot, Christophe, ed. 2007. *Hindu Nationalism – A Reader*. Princeton
University Press.

Jaffrelot, Christophe. 2008. 'Hindu Nationalism and the (Not So Easy) Art of Being
Outraged: The *Ram Setu* Controversy'. *South Asia Multidisciplinary Academic
Journal* (2). http://journals.openedition.org/samaj/1372.

Jaffrelot, Christophe. 2013. 'Refining the Moderation Thesis. Two Religious Parties
and Indian Democracy: The Jana Sangh and the BJP between Hindutva
Radicalism and Coalition Politics'. *Democratization* 20(5): 876–894.

Jaffrelot, Christophe. 2015. 'The Modi-Centric BJP 2014 Election Campaign: New
Techniques and Old Tactics'. *Contemporary Southeast Asia* 23(2): 151–166.

Jaffrelot, Christophe. 2019. 'The Fate of Secularism in India'. In *The BJP in Power:
Indian Democracy and Religious Nationalism*, ed. Milan Vaishnav. Carnegie
Endowment for International Peace, pp. 51–62.

Jaffrelot, Christophe. 2021. *Modi's India*. Princeton University Press.

Jaffrelot, Christophe, and Gilles Verniers. 2020. 'A New Party System or a New
Political System?' *Contemporary Southeast Asia* 28(2): 141–154.

Jain, Meenakshi. 2018. 'Backward Castes and Social Change in U.P. and Bihar'.
In *Caste: Its 20th Century Avatar*, ed. M. N. Srinivas. Penguin Random House
India, pp. 136–151.

Jenkins, Laura Dudley. 2003. *Identity and Identification in India: Defining the
Disadvantaged*. Routledge.

Johnson, Dennis W. 2016. *Democracy for Hire: A History of American Political
Consulting*, 1st ed. Oxford University Press.

Jones, Justin. 2019. 'Will Criminalising Triple Talaq Help India's Muslim Women?' QZ. https://qz.com/india/1709560/will-criminalising-triple-talaq-help-indias-muslim-women/ (Accessed 8 July 2020).

Kalla, Joshua L., and David E. Broockman. 2018. 'The Minimal Persuasive Effects of Campaign Contact in General Elections: Evidence from 49 Field Experiments'. *The American Political Science Review* 112(1): 148–166.

Karlsen, Rune. 2010. 'Fear of the Political Consultant: Campaign Professionals and New Technology in Norwegian Electoral Politics'. *Party Politics* 16(2): 193–214.

Kaur, Ravinder. 2016. '"I Am India Shining": The Investor-Citizen and the Indelible Icon of Good Times'. *The Journal of Asian Studies* 75(3): 621–648.

Kaviraj, Sudipta. 1988. 'A Critique of the Passive Revolution'. *Economic and Political Weekly* 23(45/47): 2429–2444.

Kaviraj, Sudipta. 2010a. *The Imaginary Institution of India: Politics and Ideas.* Columbia University Press.

Kaviraj, Sudipta. 2010b. *The Trajectories of the Indian State.* Permanent Black.

Kelkar, B. K. 2014. *Pt. Deendayal Upadhyay Ideology & Preception – Part 3: Political Thought.* Suruchi Prakashan.

Kelly, Duncan. 2017. 'Populism and the History of Popular Sovereignty'. In *The Oxford Handbook of Populism*, eds. Cristóbal Rovira Kaltwasser et al. Oxford University Press.

Kidwai, Rasheed. 2010. *24 Akbar Road.* Hachette.

Kinnvall, Catarina, and Amit Singh. 2022. 'Enforcing and Resisting Hindutva: Popular Culture, the COVID-19 Crisis and Fantasy Narratives of Motherhood and Pseudoscience in India'. *Social Sciences* 11(12): 550.

Kishor, Prashant. 'Youth in Politics'. www.youthinpolitics.in/ (Accessed 2 January 2020).

Klikauer, Thomas. 2013. 'Managerialism and Authoritarianism'. *Managerialism* 99–115. http://dx.doi.org/10.1057/9781137334275_6.

Kohli, Atul. 2009. *Democracy and Development in India : From Socialism to Pro-Business.* Oxford University Press.

Kohli, Atul. 2012. *Poverty Amid Plenty in the New India.* Cambridge University Press.

Kulkarni, Pavan. 2017. 'Deendayal Upadhyaya, Bigoted "Guiding Force" of a Hindu Rashtra'. *The Wire.* https://thewire.in/history/deendayal-upadhyaya-guiding-force-hindu-rashtra (Accessed 21 February 2022).

Lal, Vinay. 1999. 'The Politics of History on the Internet: Cyber-Diasporic Hinduism and the North American Hindu Diaspora'. *Diaspora: A Journal of Transnational Studies* 8(2): 137–172.

Li, Tania Murray. 2007. *The Will to Improve: Governmentality, Development, and the Practice of Politics.* Duke University Press.

Lisi, Marco. 2013. 'The Professionalization of Campaigns in Recent Democracies: The Portuguese Case'. *European Journal of Disorders of Communication: The Journal of the College of Speech and Language Therapists, London* 28(3): 259–276.

Ludden, David E. 2005. *Making India Hindu: Religion, Community, and the Politics of Democracy in India*. Oxford University Press.

Madhav, Ram. 2019. 'This Election Result Is a Positive Mandate in Favour of Narendra Modi'. *The Indian Express.* https://indianexpress.com/article/opin ion/columns/lok-sabha-elections-result-narendra-modi-bjp-government-con gress-5745313/ (Accessed 26 May 2019).

Malleson. 2018. 'Beyond Electoral Democracy'. *Jacobin.* www.jacobinmag.com/ 2018/05/legislature-lot-electoral-democracy-real-utopias (Accessed 28 October 2019).

Mandal, Dilip. 2019. 'Subramanian Swamy Was Right. Modi's Lateral Entry Plan Will Make Reservations Irrelevant'. *ThePrint.* https://theprint.in/opinion/sub ramanian-swamy-was-right-modis-lateral-entry-plan-will-make-reservations- irrelevant/250311/ (Accessed 21 November 2019).

Masciotra, David. 2014. 'Richard Hofstadter and America's New Wave of Anti-Intellectualism'. *The Daily Beast.* www.thedailybeast.com/articles/2014/ 03/09/richard-hofstadter-and-america-s-new-wave-of-anti-intellectualism (Accessed 23 May 2020).

Mayhew, Leon H. 1997. *The New Public: Professional Communication and the Means of Social Influence*. Cambridge University Press.

McGann, James G. 2019. *Think Tanks: The New Knowledge and Policy Brokers in Asia*. Brookings Institution Press.

McGann, James G. 2020. '2020 Global Go To Think Tank Index Report'. *TTCSP Global Go To Think Tank Index Reports.* https://repository.upenn.edu/think_ tanks/ (Accessed 3 September 2023)

McKinsey Global Institute. 2019. *Digital India.* www.mckinsey.com/~/media/ McKinsey/Business%20Functions/McKinsey%20Digital/Our%20Insights/ Digital%20India%20Technology%20to%20transform%20a%20connected% 20nation/MGI-Digital-India-Report-April-2019.ashx. (Accessed 20 July 2020)

Medvetz, Thomas. 2006. 'The Strength of Weekly Ties: Relations of Material and Symbolic Exchange in the Conservative Movement'. *Politics & Society* 34(3): 343–368.

Medvetz, Thomas. 2012a. 'Murky Power: "Think Tanks" as Boundary Organizations'. In *Rethinking Power in Organizations, Institutions, and Markets*, eds. David Courpasson, Damon Golsorkhi, and Jeffrey J. Sallaz. Emerald Group Publishing, pp. 113–133.

Medvetz, Thomas. 2012b. *Think Tanks in America*. University of Chicago Press.

Medvic, Stephen K. 2003. 'Professional Political Consultants: An Operational Definition'. *Politics* 23(2): 119–127.

Mehta, Harshil. 2020. 'New Findings at Ram Janmabhoomi Site Expose Once Again the Intellectual Dishonesty of "Eminent Experts"'. *Swarajya*. https://swarajyamag.com/blogs/new-findings-at-ram-janmabhoomi-site-expose-once-again-the-intellectual-dishonesty-of-eminent-experts (Accessed 20 March 2023).

Mehta, Mona G. 2019. Regional Liberals and the Urban Anxieties of Indian Populism'. *International Journal of Urban and Regional Research*. www.ijurr.org/spotlight-on/political-geographies-of-right-wing-populism/regional-liberals-and-the-urban-anxieties-of-indian-populism/ (Accessed 23 July 2020).

Mishra, Pankaj. 2019. 'The Secret to Modi's Success'. *Bloomberg.com*. www.bloomberg.com/opinion/articles/2019-04-14/narendra-modi-is-india-s-teflon-prime-minister (Accessed 26 April 2019).

Mitchell, Timothy. 2002. *Rule of Experts: Egypt, Techno-Politics, Modernity*. University of California Press.

Moffitt, Benjamin. 2016. *The Global Rise of Populism: Performance, Political Style, and Representation*. Stanford University Press.

Mohan, Archis. 2016. 'Demonetisation: Pune Think Tank Advised Modi, Suggested Scrapping Income Tax Too'. Business-Standard. www.business-standard.com/article/economy-policy/demonetisation-pune-think-tank-advised-modi-suggested-scrapping-income-tax-too-116111401683_1.html (Accessed 25 July 2019).

Moore, Alfred, Carlo Invernizzi-Accetti, Elizabeth Markovits, Zeynep Pamuk, et al. 2020. 'Beyond Populism and Technocracy: The Challenges and Limits of Democratic Epistemology'. *Contemporary Political Theory* 19(4). https://eprints.whiterose.ac.uk/160333/1/Moore_et_al_2020_CPT_Critical_Exchange_Final.pdf.

Mouffe, Chantal. 2005. 'The "End of Politics" and the Challenge of Right-Wing Populism'. *Populism and the Mirror of Democracy* 50–71.

Mukherji, Rahul. 2013. 'Ideas, Interests, and the Tipping Point: Economic Change in India'. *Review of International Political Economy* 20(2): 363–389.

Müller, Jan-Werner. 2016. *What Is Populism?* University of Pennsylvania Press.

Müller, Jan-Werner. 2018. 'The Rise and Rise of Populism? – OpenMind'. *OpenMind*. www.bbvaopenmind.com/en/articles/the-rise-and-rise-of-populism (Accessed 16 July 2019).

Müller, Jan-Werner. 2021. *Democracy Rules*. Farrar, Straus, and Giroux.

Naidu, M. V. 2016. 'The New Cultural Revolution: Demonetisation Is Aimed at a Behavioural Change Necessary for Building a New India'. *The Indian Express*. https://indianexpress.com/article/opinion/columns/demonetisation-effect-rbi-economy-gdp-4400464/ (Accessed December 2016).

Negrine, Ralph, Christina Holtz-Bacha, and Stylianos Papathanassopoulos. 2007. *The Professionalisation of Political Communication*. Intellect Books.

Newman, Janet, and John Clarke. 2018. 'The Instabilities of Expertise: Remaking Knowledge, Power and Politics in Unsettled Times'. *Innovation: The European Journal of Social Science Research* 31(1): 40–54.

Noorani, Abdul Gafoor Abdul. 2000. *The RSS and the BJP: A Division of Labour*. LeftWord Books.

Palshikar, Suhas. 2015. 'The BJP and Hindu Nationalism: Centrist Politics and Majoritarian Impulses'. *South Asia: Journal of South Asian Studies* 38(4): 719–735.

Palshikar, Suhas. 2017. *Electoral Politics in India*. Routledge.

Palshikar, Suhas. 2019. 'Towards Hegemony: The BJP beyond Electoral Dominance'. In *Majoritarian State: How Hindu Nationalism Is Changing India*, eds. Christophe Jaffrelot, Angana Chatterjee, and Thomas Blom Hansen. Oxford University Press, pp. 101–116.

Palshikar, Suhas. 2020. 'Politics in the Times of Hegemony'. *Seminar* 725. www.india-seminar.com/2020/725/725_suhas_palshikar.htm (Accessed 24 June 2020).

Pandian, M. S. S., and Satyaki Roy. 2014. '"Decisionism" and the Cult of Narendra Modi: A Note'. *Economic and Political Weekly* 30–31.

Pankowski, Rafal. 2010. *The Populist Radical Right in Poland: The Patriots*. Routledge.

Parsons, Craig. 2002. 'Showing Ideas as Causes: The Origins of the European Union'. *International Organization* 56(1): 47–84.

Patel, Aakar. 2022. 'Why Exactly Did Godse Kill Gandhi?' https://www.outlookindia.com/. www.outlookindia.com/website/story/why-exactly-did-godse-kill-gandhi/293200 (Accessed 21 February 2022).

Perottino, Michel, and Petra Guasti. 2020. 'Technocratic Populism à la française? The Roots and Mechanisms of Emmanuel Macron's Success'. *Politics and Governance* 8(4): 545–555.

Peters, Michael A. 2019. 'Anti-intellectualism Is a Virus'. *Educational Philosophy and Theory* 51(4): 357–363.

Pew Research Center. 2017. *Indians | Data on Asian Americans*. www.pewsocialtrends.org/fact-sheet/asian-americans-indians-in-the-u-s/ (Accessed 9 January 2020).

Pew Research Center. 2019. 'A Sampling of Public Opinion in India'. *Pew Research Center's Global Attitudes Project*. www.pewglobal.org/2019/03/25/a-sampling-of-public-opinion-in-india/ (Accessed 6 May 2019).

Pitroda, Sam. 1993. *Exploding Freedom: Roots in Technology*. Allied.

Plehwe, Dieter. 2006. *Neoliberal Hegemony: A Global Critique*, 1st ed. eds. Bernhard Walpen and Gisela Neunhöffer. Routledge.

Plehwe, Dieter. 2014. 'Think Tank Networks and the Knowledge–Interest Nexus: The Case of Climate Change'. *Critical Policy Studies* 8(1): 101–115.

Polsby, Nelson W. 1985. *Political Innovation in America: The Politics of Policy Initiation.* Yale University Press.

Pondy Lit Fest. n.d. 'The Pondy Lit Fest 2019'. *The Pondy Lit Fest 2019.* http://pondylitfest.com/ (Accessed 14 June 2020).

Postero, Nancy, and Eli Elinoff. 2019. 'Introduction: A Return to Politics'. *Anthropological Theory* 19(1): 3–28.

PTI. 2016. 'Give Me Time till December 30, I Will Give You a Clean Country: PM Modi'. *Economic Times.* https://economictimes.indiatimes.com/news/politics-and-nation/give-me-time-till-december-30-i-will-give-you-a-clean-country-pm-modi/articleshow/55398369.cms (Accessed 22 February 2022).

PTI. 2017. 'Hard Work Is More Powerful than Harvard : Modi'. *The Hindu.* www.thehindu.com/elections/uttar-pradesh-2017/hard-work-more-powerful-than-harvard-narendra-modi/article17387381.ece (Accessed 23 July 2020).

Putnam, Robert D. 1977. 'Elite Transformation in Advanced Industrial Societies: An Empirical Assessment of the Theory of Technocracy'. *Comparative Political Studies* 10(3): 383–412.

Ramachandran, Aarthi. 2004. 'Was Disbanding the Planning Commission Consultative Panels Justified?' *Business-Standard.* www.business-standard.com/article/opinion/was-disbanding-the-planning-commission-consultative-panels-justified-104101301016_1.html (Accessed 11 October 2019).

Rattanani, Jagdish. 2020. 'Ayodhya Ram Mandir: The Colour of a Conquest'. *Deccan Herald.* www.deccanherald.com/opinion/main-article/ayodhya-ram-mandir-the-colour-of-a-conquest-869638.html (Accessed 10 August 2020).

Reddy, Deepa S. 2006. *Religious Identity and Political Destiny: Hindutva in the Culture of Ethnicism.* Rowman Altamira.

Reddy, Deepa. 2011a. 'Capturing Hindutva: Rhetorics and Strategies'. *Religion Compass* 5(8): 427–438.

Reddy, Deepa. 2011b. 'Hindutva as Praxis'. *Religion Compass* 5(8): 412–426.

Reddy, Deepa S. 2018. 'What Is Neo- about Neo-Hindutva?' *Contemporary Southeast Asia* 26(4): 483–490.

Rich, Andrew. 2005. *Think Tanks, Public Policy, and the Politics of Expertise.* Cambridge University Press.

Richards, Steve. 2017. *The Rise of the Outsiders: How Mainstream Politics Lost Its Way.* Atlantic Books.

Rosanvallon, Pierre. 2011. *Democratic Legitimacy: Impartiality, Reflexivity, Proximity.* Princeton University Press.

Roy, Ananya. 2010. *Poverty Capital: Microfinance and the Making of Development.* Routledge.

Ruparelia, Sanjay. 2006. 'Rethinking Institutional Theories of Political Moderation: The Case of Hindu Nationalism in India, 1996–2004'. *Comparative Politics* 38 (3): 317–336.

Sagar. 2019. 'Narendra Modi's "Two-Caste Society" Is a Facade to Hide the BJP's Casteist Politics'. *The Caravan*. https://caravanmagazine.in/politics/narendra-modi-two-caste-society-casteist-bjp (Accessed 26 June 2019).

Saint-Martin, Denis. 2004. 'Building the New Managerialist State: Consultants and the Politics of Public Sector Reform in Comparative Perspective'. *OUP Catalogue*. https://ideas.repec.org/b/oxp/obooks/9780199269068.html (Accessed 25 October 2019).

Sanyal, Kalyan. 2007. *Rethinking Capitalist Development: Primitive Accumulation, Governmentality and Post-Colonial Capitalism*. Routledge India.

Sarayu Trust. 2018. 'Hindu Charter of Demands – Seeking Equal Rights for Hindus of India'. *Sarayu Trust*. https://sarayutrust.org/hindu-charter-of-demands-seeking-equal-rights-for-hindus-of-india/ (Accessed 21 February 2022).

Sarkar, Pooja. n.d. 'Political Strategists: The Campaign Makers | Forbes India'. *Forbes India*. www.forbesindia.com/article/poll-vault/political-strategists-the-campaign-makers/52793/1 (Accessed 11 June 2019).

Schedler, Andreas. 2016. *The End of Politics?: Explorations into Modern Antipolitics*. Springer.

Schildt, Henri, Saku Mantere, and Joep Cornelissen. 2019. 'Power in Sensemaking Processes'. *Organization Studies* 41(2): 241–265.

Schnapper, Dominique, and Roger Greaves. 1994. 'The Significance of the Ethnoreligious Field in Nation-Building'. *International Journal of Sociology of the Family* 24(2/3): 61–80.

Shamsul-islam. 2010. *RSS Primer: Based on Rashtriya Swayamsevak Sangh Documents*. Pharos Media & Publishing Pvt Ltd.

Sharma, Amogh Dhar. 2022. '"Mr. Clean" and His "Computer Boys": Technology, Technocracy, and De-politicisation in the Indian National Congress (1981–1991)'. *Commonwealth & Comparative Politics* 60(1): 50–73.

Sharma, Manoj. 2018. 'Meet the Backroom Boys Who Add a Spin to Election Battles'. https://www.hindustantimes.com/. www.hindustantimes.com/delhi-news/meet-the-backroom-boys-who-add-a-spin-to-election-battle/story-kK8eAcBgPEdsUEgwt4uavM.html (Accessed 11 June 2019).

Sheingate, Adam. 2016. *Building a Business of Politics: The Rise of Political Consulting and the Transformation of American Democracy (Studies in Postwar American Political Development)*, 1st ed. Oxford University Press.

Shrikanth, Siddarth. 2019. 'Government Use of Consultants Soars in India'. *Financial Times*. www.ft.com/content/76f530ae-787e-11e9-b0ec-7dff87b9a4a2 (Accessed 1 July 2019).

Siddiqui, Kalim. 2012. 'Developing Countries' Experience with Neoliberalism and Globalisation'. *Research in Applied Economics* 4(4): 12–37.

Siddiqui, Kalim. 2017. 'Hindutva, Neoliberalism and the Reinventing of India'. *Journal of Economic and Social Thought* 4(2): 142–186.

Singh, Angad. 2020. 'Why Modi Inaugurated a Temple Being Built over a Razed Mosque on the Kashmir Crackdown Anniversary'. *Vice.* www.vice.com/en_us/article/xg87jj/why-modi-is-building-a-temple-over-a-razed-mosque-on-the-kashmir-crackdown-anniversary (Accessed 11 August 2020).

Singh, Shivam Shankar. 2019. *How to Win an Indian Election: What Political Parties Don't Want You to Know.* Penguin Random House India.

Sinha, Arunav. 2014. 'Political Consultancy Firms May Rake in Rs 700–800 Crore in Poll Campaign Strategy and Management: ASSOCHAM'. *Times of India.* https://timesofindia.indiatimes.com/news/political-consultancy-firms-may-rake-in-rs-700-800-crore-in-poll-campaign-strategy-and-management-assocham/articleshow/33921949.cms (Accessed 23 February 2022).

Sircar, Neelanjan. 2020. 'The Politics of Vishwas: Political Mobilization in the 2019 National Election'. *Contemporary Southeast Asia* 28(2): 178–194.

Sivaramakrishnan, Arvind. 2012. *Public Policy and Citizenship: Battling Managerialism in India.* SAGE Publishing India.

Skocpol, Theda, and Vanessa Williamson. 2016. *The Tea Party and the Remaking of Republican Conservatism.* Oxford University Press.

Southern Poverty Law Center. n.d. 'Alt-Right'. *Southern Poverty Law Center.* www.splcenter.org/fighting-hate/extremist-files/ideology/alt-right (Accessed 20 June 2020).

Springborg, Patricia. 1984. 'Karl Marx on Democracy, Participation, Voting, and Equality'. *Political Theory* 12(4): 537–556.

Srinivasaraju, Sugata. 2019. 'The Trap of the Lutyens Liberal'. *The Wire.* https://thewire.in/rights/india-liberalism-lutyens-regional (Accessed 12 July 2023)

Strömbäck, Jesper. 2009. 'Selective Professionalisation of Political Campaigning: A Test of the Party-Centred Theory of Professionalised Campaigning in the Context of the 2006 Swedish Election'. *Political Studies* 57(1): 95–116.

Sud, Nikita. 2022. 'The Actual Gujarat Model: Authoritarianism, Capitalism, Hindu Nationalism and Populism in the Time of Modi'. *Journal of Contemporary Asia* 52(1): 102–126.

Suri, K. C., and Rahul Verma. 2017. 'Democratizing the BJP'. In *Seminar*, pp. 26–30. www.india-seminar.com/2017/699/699_k_c_suri-rahul_verma.htm (Accessed April 2020).

Swyngedouw, Erik. 2010. 'Apocalypse Forever?' *Theory, Culture & Society* 27(2–3): 213–232.

Thachil, Tariq. 2014. *Elite Parties, Poor Voters: How Social Services Win Votes in India*. Cambridge University Press.

Thacker, Teena et al. 2018. 'Kumbh Mela: How UP Will Manage One of the World's Biggest Religious Festival'. *The Economic Times*. https://economictimes .indiatimes.com/news/politics-and-nation/kumbh-mela-how-up-will-manage-one-of-the-worlds-biggest-religious-festival/articleshow/67177421.cms (Accessed 9 May 2020).

Thakur, By Sankarshan. 2016. 'The Unravelling of Prashant Kishor'. *Telegraph India*. www.telegraphindia.com/7-days/the-unravelling-of-nbsp-prashant-kishor/cid/ 1314336 (Accessed 19 June 2019).

Therwath, Ingrid. 2012. 'Cyber-Hindutva: Hindu Nationalism, the Diaspora and the Web'. *Social Sciences Information. Information sur les sciences sociales* 51 (4): 551–577.

Thompson, Barbara. 2016. *Neoliberalism, New Managerialism, Policies and Practices*. Palgrave.

Times of India. 2020. 'What Is CAA?' *Times of India*. https://timesofindia .indiatimes.com/india/what-is-caa/articleshow/73153785.cms (Accessed 21 February 2022).

Times of India. 2022. 'UP Election 2022: For Us, Goa Means Governance, Opportunities, Aspirations, Says PM Modi'. *Times of India*. https:// timesofindia.indiatimes.com/india/up-elections-2022-phase-1-voting-yogi-adi tyanath-priyanka-gandhi-akhilesh-yadav/liveblog/89462337.cms (Accessed 11 February 2022).

Tribe, Laurence. 1972. 'Policy Science: Analysis or Ideology?' *Philosophy and Public Affairs* 2(1): 66–110.

Udupa, Sahana. 2015. 'Internet Hindus: New India's Ideological Warriors'. In *Handbook of Religion in Asian Cities*, University of California Press, pp. 432–451.

Udupa, Sahana. 2018a. 'Enterprise Hindutva and Social Media in Urban India'. *Contemporary Southeast Asia* 26(4): 453–467.

Udupa, Sahana. 2018b. 'Gaali Cultures: The Politics of Abusive Exchange on Social Media'. *New Media & Society* 20(4): 1506–1522.

Udupa, Sahana. 2018c. *Making News in Global India: Media, Publics, Politics*. Cambridge University Press.

Upadhyay, Ashok. 2018. '10 Things Ambedkar Said in His Lifetime that BJP Wouldn't Bear to Hear'. *Daily O*. www.dailyo.in/politics/bjp-appropiating-br-ambedkar-uttar-pradesh-yogi-aditayanth-dalits-hinduism-hindutva/story/1/ 23391.html (Accessed 7 May 2020).

Urbinati, Nadia. 2019. 'Political Theory of Populism'. *Annual Review of Political Science* 22(1): 111–127.

Vaishnav, Milan. 2019. 'Religious Nationalism and India's Future'. In *The BJP in Power: Indian Democracy and Religious Nationalism*. Carnegie Endowment for International Peace Publications Department.

van der Veer, Peter. 2007. 'Global Breathing: Religious Utopias in India and China'. *Anthropological Theory* 7(3): 315–328.

Van Dijk, Teun A. 2006. 'Ideology and Discourse Analysis'. *Journal of Political Ideologies* 11(2): 115–140.

Vanaik, Achin. 2017. *The Rise of Hindu Authoritarianism: Secular Claims, Communal Realities*. Verso.

Vanaik, Achin. 2018. 'India's Two Hegemonies'. *New Left Review* 112. https://newleftreview.org/II/112/achin-vanaik-india-s-two-hegemonies (Accessed 14 September 2018).

Varshney, Ashutosh. 2014. 'Modi the Moderate'. The Indian Express. https://indianexpress.com/article/opinion/columns/modi-the-moderate/ (Accessed April 2019).

Verma, Rahul. 2019. 'The Emergence, Stagnation, and Ascendance of the BJP'. In *The BJP in Power: Indian Democracy and Religious Nationalism*, ed. Milan Vaishnav. Carnegie Endowment for International Peace, pp. 23–36.

Verniers, Gilles. 2019. 'Breaking Down the Uttar Pradesh Verdict: In Biggest Bout, Knockout'. *The Indian Express*. https://indianexpress.com/article/explained/lok-sabha-elections-uttar-pradesh-bjp-modi-amit-shah-yogi-5751375/ (Accessed 23 July 2020).

Verniers, Gilles, and Christophe Jaffrelot. 2020. 'The Reconfiguration of India's Political Elite: Profiling the 17th Lok Sabha'. *Contemporary Southeast Asia* 28(2): 242–254.

Von Mises, Ludwig, and Bettina Bien Greaves. 1944. *Bureaucracy*. Yale University Press New Haven.

Weber, Max. 1958. *Essays in Sociology*. A Galaxy Book.

Wedel, Janine R., Cris Shore, Gregory Feldman, and Stacy Lathrop. 2005. 'Toward an Anthropology of Public Policy'. *The Annals of the American Academy of Political and Social Science* 600(1): 30–51.

Winch, Peter. 2008. *The Idea of a Social Science and Its Relation to Philosophy*. Routledge.

Wodak, Ruth. 2015. *The Politics of Fear*. Sage.

Yadav, Jyoti. 2020. 'Kapil Mishra to Payal Rohatgi, India's New 'Intellectuals' Are Dethroning One Guha at a Time'. *ThePrint*. https://theprint.in/opinion/pov/kapil-mishra-to-payal-rohatgi-indias-new-intellectuals-are-dethroning-one-guha-at-a-time/438833/ (Accessed 11 June 2020).

Yengde, Suraj. 2019. *Caste Matters*. Penguin Random House India.

Index

Accetti, Carlo Invernizzi, 6–7
Adityanath, Yogi, 158–159
Advani, L. K., 1, 41–42, 49
advertising agencies, 117–118
Ambani, Mukesh, 79–81
Ambedkar, B. R., 36–37, 64, 73–74
Anderson, Edward, 24
anti-corruption movement, 47, 53, 164
    BJP anti-corruption discourse, 49–50,
        53–55
anti-intellectualism, 5, 39, 60–62, 72–73, 88
anti-political actors, typology, 163–165
Association of a Billion Minds, 127–129
Aurobindo, Sri, 149

Babri Masjid mosque, 1–2, 41–42
Baxter, Leone, 114
Bharat, Atmanirbhar, 25
Bharatiya Jana Sangh, 23, 30–32
Bharatiya Janata Party (BJP)
    adoption of liberal intellectual culture,
        140
    Alt Right politics, 60–62
    anti-corruption discourse, 49–50, 53–55
    anti-intellectualism, 39, 60–61, 72–73,
        164–165
    approach to dissent and external critique,
        134, 166
    attacks on Congress Party, 49–50, 53–55,
        151
    building of New Elite, 72–73
    demonetisation, 54–58
    development-focused narratives, 35–40
    disbanding of Planning Commission,
        67–68, 95
    election campaigns
        2004 national election, 45, 117–118
        2014 national election, 3, 19, 28–29,
            77, 106, 122–123, 153
        2019 national election, 3, 28–30, 35,
            48, 77, 127–129, 153
        state elections, 35, 38, 52
    fellowship programmes, 140–141

Hindu nationalism. *See also* Hindutva
    basis of ideology, 28–34
    and development, 35–40
    double-sidedness of, 48, 135–141
    and economic policy,
        24–25
    equated with Indian way of life,
        22–23
    heterodoxy, 24–25
    public acceptance of, 20–21
    Ram Mandir movement, 1–4, 41–42,
        138
    version of Alt Right, 60–62
    violence against minorities, 17, 44
    lateral entry to IAS, 106
    manufacture of moral panics,
        32–33
    multiple narratives and alternative
        logics, 17–19
    in opposition 2009–2014, 46–47, 68
    relationship with RSS, 17, 32, 71
    role in Ram Mandir movement, 1, 3,
        42–43
    shifts in social and economic policy,
        40–53
    social base, 23, 38, 43, 47, 61–62, 165
    social media campaigns, 28–30, 38
    techno-populism, 8–12, 17–25
    use of think tanks, 77–78, 81, 83, 87–92,
        134–137, 139–141. *See also*
        Chanakya Institute (CI); India
        Foundation (IF); Vivekananda
        International Foundation (VIF)
    welfare programmes, 47–48, 83
Bharti, Nitin Kumar, 58
Bickerton, Christopher, 6–7
Bihar state elections, 129–130
BJP. *See* Bharatiya Janata Party (BJP)
Bokil, Anil, 58
Brahmanical knowledge production, 81
Brahmins, 30, 58–59. *See also* upper castes
British colonial impact, 27–28
Brown, Wendy, 138

bureaucracy
  attitudes towards, 105
  literature on, 102–103

Candea, Matei, 138
caste system, 23, 58–59, 61–62
Chakravartty, Paula, 104
Chakravarty, Praveen, 88
Chanakya Institute (CI), 134, 136–137,
    141–149, 153, 155–161
Chandrashekhar, 42
Charter of Hindu Demands (2018), 26–27
Chatterjee, Partha, 67, 100, 149
Chaturvedi, Swati, 62
Chhibber, Pradeep, 10–11
Citizen's Alliance, 123
Citizens for Accountable Governance (CAG),
    121–123
Clarke, John, 103
Congress Party
  BJP discourses against, 49–50, 53–55, 151
  caste representation, 165
  election campaigns, 21, 45, 117
  participation of civil society groups,
      133–134
  periods in office, 41–43, 45–46
  response to construction of Ram Mandir,
      2–3
Constitution of India
  Article 370 (Kashmir), 21, 26
  RSS criticism of, 33, 35–37
  voting system, 116
consulting firms, 100–102, 107–112. See also
    political consultants

Dalits, 23, 33–34, 43, 58–59. See also
    Scheduled Castes (SC)
Das, Subhash, 149–151, 154
Dasgupta, Swapan, 48–49, 60–62, 87–89, 141
Davies, William, 21–22
demonetisation (2016), 54–58
Desai, Ashok, 11
Desai, Radhika, 40, 148
Dubey, Amber, 109

election market, 99–101, 109–110, 126–127.
    See also political consultants
Elst, Koenraad, 155
entrepreneurial citizenship model, 165
Ernst & Young, 36

Ferguson, James, 138
Five Star Movement (M5S), 8
Foucault, Michel, 102

Gandhi, Indira, 84
Gandhi, Mahatma, 30–31
  appropriation of image, 36–37, 55–56
Gandhi, Rajiv, 41–42, 117
Ganguly, Anirban, 91–92
Ghar Wapsi rallies, 22–23
Goa state elections, 35
Gogoi, Ranjan, 1–2
Golwalkar, M. S., 30–31, 33, 52
Goswami, Arnab, 38
Govindacharya, K. N., 43
Gramscian hegemony, 140, 147–148, 157
Grey Worldwide, 117–118
Gudavarthy, Ajay, 59
Guha, Ramachandra, 11
Gujarat Pogrom, 44
Gupta, Akhil, 102–103
Gupta, Rajendra Pratap, 106

Hall, Stuart, 32–33, 37, 162
Hansen, Thomas Blom, 65–66, 138, 164
Hasan, Nafis A, 98
Havelka, Miloš, 16
Hazare, Anna, 47, 164
Herzfeld, Michael, 103
Hindutva
  basis of ideology, 28–34
  on colonisation, 27–28, 148–149
  and development, 35–40
  double-sidedness of, 48, 135–141
  foundational thinkers, 30
  heterodoxy, 24–25
  in the Independence movement, 20
  as mediating discourse of social
      life, 19
  narratives of persecution, 56
  origin and meaning of term, 9, 22, 30
  Ram Mandir movement, 1–4, 41–42, 138
  relation to technocracy, 88–92
  scholarship on, 137
  version of Alt Right, 60–62
  violence against minorities, 17, 33–34
Hodge, Bob, 139
Hofstadter, Richard, 5
Honig, Dan, 112
Howarth, David, 86

ideology, use of term, 123–124
India Foundation (IF), 81–82, 87, 134,
    136–137, 149–154, 157–161
Indian Administrative Services (IAS),
    105–106, 109
Indian constitution. *See* Constitution of India
Indian diaspora, 153–155
Indian national elections
    1989 election, 117
    1999 election, 44
    2004 election, 44–45, 117–118
    2014 election, 3, 19, 28–29, 77, 94, 106,
        120–123, 153
    2019 election, 3, 21–22, 28–30, 35, 48, 52,
        77, 127–129, 153
Indian Political Action Committee (IPAC),
    120–121, 129–130
Indian School of Public Policy (ISPP), 111
intellectuals
    influence of, 28, 67
    opposition to, 5, 39, 60–62, 72–73, 88
    in relation to professionals, 98
Interactive Voice Response calls, 128–129
Irani, Lilly, 47, 97, 131, 165
Irani, Smriti, 39

Jaffrelot, Christophe, 73
Jana Sangh. *See* Bharatiya Jana Sangh
Janata Dal (United) (JDU), 129–130
Jarvis Consulting, 120, 127–129
Jawaharlal Nehru University, 39, 144

Kashmir, 21, 36
Kathuria, Rajat, 86
Kautilya Fellows Programme, 87, 157
Kaviraj, Sudipta, 66, 104
Kishor, Prashant, 100–101, 121–126, 129–130
Kovind, Ram Nath, 2
Kumar, Nitish, 129–130
Kumbh Mela 2019, 36

La République En Marche (LREM), 7–8
lateral entry to IAS, 105–106, 109
liberalisation of economy, 40–41, 44–45,
    66–67
Lokpal movement, 47, 53, 164
Longkumer, Arkotong, 24

Macron, Emmanuel, 7–8
Madhav, Ram, 21–22, 51–52, 78, 81, 159–160

Malhotra, Rajiv, 155
management consultants. *See* consulting
    firms
managerialism, 103–104
Mandal Commission, 43
Mayhew, Leon H, 118
Mishra, Pankaj, 38
Modi, Narendra
    as BJP prime ministerial candidate 2014,
        47, 50
    campaigns to Indian diaspora, 153–154
    caste rhetoric, 164–165
    as Chief Minister of Gujarat, 44, 99, 154
    citizen as stakeholder discourse, 50–53
    Covid-era rhetoric, 25, 162
    development rhetoric, 68–69, 138
    distaste for intellectuals, liberals and
        critics, 60
    election campaigning, 19, 21–22, 35,
        38–39, 127
    ground-breaking of Ram Mandir site,
        2
    parliamentary speeches, 36
    public profile and persona, 37–39, 56–58
    social media use, 38
    Swachh Bharat campaign, 37
    use of Congress Party and Gandhi
        narratives, 55–56
    victory speech 2019, 48
moral panics, 32–33
Müller, Jan-Werner, 63
Muslims
    criminalising of triple talaq, 20–21
    destruction of Babri Masjid mosque, 1–2,
        41–42
    violence against, 21–23, 33–34, 44
Mussolini, Benito, 7

Naidu, Venkaiah, 54–55
National Advisory Council (NAC), 46
national elections. *See* Indian national
    elections
National Front, 42
Nayyar, Dhiraj, 50–51, 53
Nazi Party, RSS admiration of, 31
Newman, Janet, 103
NITI Aayog, 67–68, 88–89, 95, 136

objective intellectual model, 164–165
Observer Research Foundation (ORF), 79–81

Other Backward Classes (OBCs), 23, 43, 58–59, 61
outsourcing. *See* consulting firms; political consultants; think tanks; think tanks (BJP affiliated)

Palshikar, Suhas, 17–18, 134
Patra, Sambit, 36
Pitroda, Sam, 67
Planning Commission (PC), 67–68, 95, 104–105, 133
policy making
    rationale, 99–100
    in relation to politics, 63, 65, 85, 96, 150–151
policy market, 99, 109–110. *See also* consulting firms
political ascetic model, 163–164
political consultants, 113–131
    growth of, 114, 120–123
    impact on democracy, 100–101, 116–118, 126–127
    recruitment and motivation, 123–126
    reliance on data analytics, 115–116
    role of, 114–115, 117, 126–131
    use of social media, 118–120
Political Edge, consulting firm, 121
Pondicherry Lit Fest, 149
populism
    as break from constitutional democracy, 64
    multiple frameworks of, 68–69
    relation to technocracy, 4–9, 62–63
post-ideology, 83–85, 89, 123–124
Pritchett, Lant, 107, 112

Ram Mandir movement, 1–4, 41–42, 138
Ramesh, Jairam, 83–85
Rao, P. V. Narasimha, 43
Rao, Sachin, 74–75, 116, 126–127
Rashtriya Swayamsevak Sangh (RSS).
    See also Sangh Parivar
    calls for demolition of Babri Masjid mosque, 1, 43
    foundational thinkers, 30, 52
    ideology, 30–32
    multiple positionings, 22–24, 138
    position on Indian Constitution, 33
    relationship with BJP, 17, 32, 71

shifts in social and economic policy, 40–53
    use of violence, 17, 22–23
Reddy, Deepa S, 27, 48, 135–136, 138–139, 161
Rediffusion, 117
RSS. *See* Rashtriya Swayamsevak Sangh (RSS)

Samajwadi Party, 117
Sangh Parivar, 1, 24–28. *See also* Bharatiya Janata Party (BJP); Rashtriya Swayamsevak Sangh (RSS); Vishwa Hindu Parishad (VHP)
Sanyal, Kalyan, 47
Savarkar, VD, 9, 22, 30
Scheduled Castes (SC), 58–59, 61. *See also* Dalits
Scheduled Tribes (ST), 43, 58–59, 61
Sen, Amartya, 60
Sikhs, violence against, 23
Singh, Manmohan, 46
Singh, V. P., 42
Sircar, Neelanjan, 52
social media use, 28–30, 34, 38, 118–120, 128–129
Spencer, Richard, 60–61
Srinivasaraju, Sugata, 26–27
state elections, 21, 35, 38, 52
Swachh Bharat campaign, 37
Swadeshi Jagran Manch, 83
Swyngedouw, Erik, 85

technocracy
    growth of in India, 85–87
    origin of term, 69
    relation to Hindu nationalism, 88–92
    relation to populism, 4–9, 62–63
techno-populism, concept of, 6–7, 104
Thatcher, Margaret, 7, 32–33
think tanks
    claims to credibility, 82–83
    consulting firms contrasted, 101–102
    defining impact of, 69–77
    meaning and use of term, 12, 78–79
    rise of think tank governance, 66–69, 78–79
    role in disseminating ideas, 82
    scholarship on, 69–70
    typology of, 79–81

think tanks (BJP affiliated), 77–78, 81, 83,
        87–92, 134–137, 139–141,
        156–157. *See also* Chanakya
        Institute (CI); India Foundation
        (IF); Vivekananda International
        Foundation (VIF)
Times of India, 1, 35
triple talaq, 20–21
Trump, Donald, 142, 154
Tukde Tukde Gang, 39

Udupa, Sahana, 62
United States, Indian diaspora, 153–155
Upadhyay, Deendayal, 30–32, 52
upper castes, 58, 61
Urbinati, Nadia, 33, 69
Uttar Pradesh, 29, 36–38, 117. *See also* Ram
        Mandir movement
Uttarakhand state elections, 38

Vadra, Priyanka Gandhi, 3
Vajpayee, Atal Bihari, 40–41, 44
van der Veer, Peter, 163
Van Dijk, Teun A, 164
Vanaik, Achin, 28
Verma, Rahul, 10–11, 19
Verniers, Gilles, 73
Vishwa Hindu Parishad (VHP), 41
Vivekananda International Foundation, 81,
        90–91
Von Mises, Ludwig, 105

WarRoom Strategies, consulting firm, 121
Whitaker, Clem, 114
Winch, Peter, 112

Youth in Politics (YIP), 125

Zainulbhai, Adil, 109

9 781009 349758